MOS 2013 Study Guide
for Microsoft Word

Joan Lambert

PUBLISHED BY
Microsoft Press
A Division of Microsoft Corporation
One Microsoft Way
Redmond, Washington 98052-6399

Library of Congress Control Number: 2013939519
ISBN: 978-0-7356-6925-3

Printed and bound in the United States of America.

Sixth Printing: September 2015

Microsoft Press books are available through booksellers and distributors worldwide. If you need support related to this book, email Microsoft Press Book Support at mspinput@microsoft.com. Please tell us what you think of this book at http://www.microsoft.com/learning/booksurvey.

Acquisitions Editor: Rosemary Caperton
Editorial Production: Online Training Solutions, Inc. (OTSI)
Technical Reviewer: Rob Carr (OTSI)
Copyeditor: Kathy Krause (OTSI)
Indexers: Candace Sinclair and Joan Lambert (OTSI)
Cover: Microsoft Press Brand Team

Contents

What do you think of this book? We want to hear from you!

Microsoft is interested in hearing your feedback so we can continually improve our books and learning resources for you. To participate in a brief online survey, please visit:

microsoft.com/learning/booksurvey

2   Format text, paragraphs, and sections   61

5   Insert and format objects   135

Introduction

The Microsoft Office Specialist (MOS) certification program has been designed to validate your knowledge of and ability to use programs in the Microsoft Office 2013 suite of programs, Microsoft Office 365, and Microsoft SharePoint. This book has been designed to guide you in studying the types of tasks you are likely to be required to demonstrate in Exam 77-418: Microsoft Word 2013.

> **See Also** For information about the tasks you are likely to be required to demonstrate in Exam 77-419: Microsoft Word 2013 Expert, see *MOS 2013 Study Guide for Microsoft Word Expert* by John Pierce (Microsoft Press, 2013).

Who this book is for

MOS 2013 Study Guide for Microsoft Word is designed for experienced computer users seeking Microsoft Office Specialist certification in Word 2013.

MOS exams for individual programs are practical rather than theoretical. You must demonstrate that you can complete certain tasks or projects rather than simply answering questions about program features. The successful MOS certification candidate will have at least six months of experience using all aspects of the application on a regular basis; for example, using Word at work or school to create and manage documents, format document content, present information in tables and lists, insert and format pictures, create business diagrams, and reference sources.

As a certification candidate, you probably have a lot of experience with the program you want to become certified in. Many of the procedures described in this book will be familiar to you; others might not be. Read through each study section and ensure that you are familiar with not only the procedures included in the section, but also the concepts and tools discussed in the review information. In some cases, graphics depict the tools you will use to perform procedures related to the skill set. Study the graphics and ensure that you are familiar with all the options available for each tool.

How this book is organized

The exam coverage is divided into chapters representing broad skill sets that correlate to the functional groups covered by the exam, and each chapter is divided into sections addressing groups of related skills that correlate to the exam objectives. Each section includes review information, generic procedures, and practice tasks you can complete on your own while studying. When necessary, we provide practice files you can use to work through the practice tasks. You can practice the procedures in this book by using the practice files supplied or by using your own files. (If you use your own files, keep in mind that functionality in Word 2013 is limited in files created in or saved for earlier versions of the program. When you are working in such a file, *Compatibility Mode* appears in the program window title bar.)

Throughout this book, you will find Strategy tips that present information about the scope of study that is necessary to ensure that you achieve mastery of a skill set and are successful in your certification effort.

Download the practice files

Before you can complete the practice tasks in this book, you need to download the book's practice files to your computer. These practice files can be downloaded from the following page:

http://aka.ms/mosWord2013/files

> **Important** The Word 2013 program is not available from this website. You should purchase and install that program before using this book.

If you would like to be able to refer to the completed versions of practice files at a later time, you can save the practice files that you modify while working through the exercises in this book. If you save your changes and later want to repeat the exercise, you can download the original practice files again.

The following table lists the practice files for this book.

Folder and functional group	Files
MOSWord2013\Objective1 1 Create and manage documents	*Word_1-1a.dotx* *Word_1-1b.txt* *Word_1-1c.pdf* *Word_1-2.docx* *Word_1-3a.docx* *Word_1-3b.docx* *Word_1-4a.docx* *Word_1-4b.docx* *Word_1-4c.docx* *Word_1-5a.docx* *Word_1-5b.docx* *Word_1-5c.docx*
MOSWord2013\Objective2 2 Format text, paragraphs, and sections	*Word_2-1a.docx* *Word_2-1b.pptx* *Word_2-1c.docx* *Word_2-2.docx* *Word_2-3.docx*
MOSWord2013\Objective3 3 Create tables and lists	*Word_3-1.docx* *Word_3-2a.docx* *Word_3-2b.docx* *Word_3-3.docx*
MOSWord2013\Objective4 4 Apply references	*Word_4-1.docx* *Word_4-2.docx*
MOSWord2013\Objective5 5 Insert and format objects	*Word_5-1.docx* *Word_5-2.docx* *Word_5-3a.docx* *Word_5-3b.jpg*

Adapting exercise steps

The screen images shown in this book were captured at a screen resolution of 1024 × 768, at 100 percent magnification. If your settings are different, the ribbon on your screen might not look the same as the one shown in this book. For example, you might have more or fewer buttons in each of the groups, the buttons you have might be represented by larger or smaller icons than those shown, or the group might be represented by a button that you click to display the group's commands. As a result, exercise instructions that involve the ribbon might require a little adaptation. Our instructions use this format:

→ On the **Insert** tab, in the **Illustrations** group, click the **Chart** button.

If the command is in a list or on a menu, our instructions use this format:

→ On the **Home** tab, in the **Editing** group, click the **Find** arrow and then, on the **Find** menu, click **Advanced Find**.

> **Tip** On subsequent instances of instructions located on the same tab or in the same group, the instructions are simplified to reflect that we've already established the working location.

If differences between your display settings and ours cause a button to appear differently on your screen than it does in this book, you can easily adapt the steps to locate the command. First click the specified tab, and then locate the specified group. If a group has been collapsed into a group list or under a group button, click the list or button to display the group's commands. If you can't immediately identify the button you want, point to likely candidates to display their names in ScreenTips.

If you prefer not to have to adapt the steps, set up your screen to match ours while you read and work through the exercises in this book.

In this book, we provide instructions based on the traditional keyboard and mouse input methods. If you're using the program on a touch-enabled device, you might be giving commands by tapping with a stylus or your finger. If so, substitute a tapping action any time we instruct you to click a user interface element. Also note that when we tell you to enter information, you can do so by typing on a keyboard, tapping an on-screen keyboard, or even speaking aloud, depending on your computer setup and your personal preferences.

Ebook edition

If you're reading the ebook edition of this book, you can do the following:

- Search the full text
- Print
- Copy and paste

You can purchase and download the ebook edition from our Microsoft Press site at oreilly.com, which you can find at:

http://aka.ms/mosWord2013

Get support and give feedback

The following sections provide information about getting help with this book and contacting us to provide feedback or report errors.

Errata

We've made every effort to ensure the accuracy of this book and its companion content. Any errors that have been reported since this book was published are listed on our Microsoft Press site:

http://aka.ms/mosWord2013/errata

If you find an error that is not already listed, you can report it to us through the same page.

If you need additional support, email Microsoft Press Book Support at:

mspinput@microsoft.com

Please note that product support for Microsoft software is not offered through the preceding addresses.

We want to hear from you

At Microsoft Press, your satisfaction is our top priority, and your feedback our most valuable asset. Please tell us what you think of this book at:

http://www.microsoft.com/learning/booksurvey

The survey is short, and we read every one of your comments and ideas. Thanks in advance for your input!

Stay in touch

Let's keep the conversation going! We're on Twitter at:

http://twitter.com/MicrosoftPress

Taking a Microsoft Office Specialist exam

Desktop computing proficiency is increasingly important in today's business world. When screening, hiring, and training employees, employers can feel reassured by relying on the objectivity and consistency of technology certification to ensure the competence of their workforce. As an employee or job seeker, you can use technology certification to prove that you already have the skills you need to succeed, saving current and future employers the time and expense of training you.

Microsoft Office Specialist certification

Microsoft Office Specialist certification is designed to assist employees in validating their skills with Office programs. The following certification paths are available:

- A Microsoft Office Specialist (MOS) is an individual who has demonstrated proficiency by passing a certification exam in one or more Office programs, including Microsoft Word, Excel, PowerPoint, Outlook, Access, OneNote, or SharePoint.

- A Microsoft Office Specialist Expert (MOS Expert) is an individual who has taken his or her knowledge of Office to the next level and has demonstrated by passing a certification exam that he or she has mastered the more advanced features of Word or Excel.

Selecting a certification path

When deciding which certifications you would like to pursue, you should assess the following:

- The program and program version(s) with which you are familiar
- The length of time you have used the program and how frequently you use it
- Whether you have had formal or informal training in the use of that program
- Whether you use most or all of the available program features
- Whether you are considered a go-to resource by business associates, friends, and family members who have difficulty with the program

Candidates for MOS-level certification are expected to successfully complete a wide range of standard business tasks, such as formatting a document or worksheet and its content; creating and formatting visual content; or working with SharePoint lists, libraries, Web Parts, and dashboards. Successful candidates generally have six or more months of experience with the specific Office program, including either formal, instructor-led training or self-study using MOS-approved books, guides, or interactive computer-based materials.

Candidates for MOS Expert–level certification are expected to successfully complete more complex tasks that involve using the advanced functionality of the program. Successful candidates generally have at least six months, and may have several years, of experience with the programs, including formal, instructor-led training or self-study using MOS-approved materials.

Test-taking tips

Every MOS certification exam is developed from a set of exam skill standards (referred to as the objective domain) that are derived from studies of how the Office programs are used in the workplace. Because these skill standards dictate the scope of each exam, they provide critical information about how to prepare for certification. This book follows the structure of the published exam objectives; see "How this book is organized" in the Introduction for more information.

The MOS certification exams are performance based and require you to complete business-related tasks or projects in the program for which you are seeking certification. For example, you might be presented with a file and told to do something specific with it, or presented with a sample document and told to create it by using resources provided for that purpose. Your score on the exam reflects how well you perform the requested tasks or complete the project within the allotted time.

Here is some helpful information about taking the exam:

- Keep track of the time. Your exam time does not officially begin until after you finish reading the instructions provided at the beginning of the exam. During the exam, the amount of time remaining is shown at the bottom of the exam interface. You can't pause the exam after you start it.

- Pace yourself. At the beginning of the exam, you will receive information about the questions or projects that are included in the exam. Some questions will require that you complete more than one task. Each project will require that you complete multiple tasks. During the exam, the amount of time remaining to complete the questions or project, and the number of completed and remaining questions if applicable, is shown at the bottom of the exam interface.

- Read the exam instructions carefully before beginning. Follow all the instructions provided completely and accurately.

- Enter requested information as it appears in the instructions, but without duplicating the formatting unless you are specifically instructed to do so. For example, the text and values you are asked to enter might appear in the instructions in bold and underlined text, but you should enter the information without applying these formats.

- Close all dialog boxes before proceeding to the next exam question unless you are specifically instructed not to do so.

- Don't close task panes before proceeding to the next exam question unless you are specifically instructed not to do so.

- If you are asked to print a document, worksheet, chart, report, or slide, perform the task, but be aware that nothing will actually be printed.

- When performing tasks to complete a project-based exam, save your work frequently.

- Don't worry about extra keystrokes or mouse clicks. Your work is scored based on its result, not on the method you use to achieve that result (unless a specific method is indicated in the instructions).

- If a computer problem occurs during the exam (for example, if the exam does not respond or the mouse no longer functions) or if a power outage occurs, contact a testing center administrator immediately. The administrator will restart the computer and return the exam to the point where the interruption occurred, with your score intact.

> **Strategy** This book includes special tips for effectively studying for the Microsoft Office Specialist exams in Strategy paragraphs such as this one.

Certification benefits

At the conclusion of the exam, you will receive a score report, indicating whether you passed the exam. If your score meets or exceeds the passing standard (the minimum required score), you will be contacted by email by the Microsoft Certification Program team. The email message you receive will include your Microsoft Certification ID and links to online resources, including the Microsoft Certified Professional site. On this site, you can download or order a printed certificate, create a virtual business card, order an ID card, view and share your certification transcript, access the Logo Builder, and access other useful and interesting resources, including special offers from Microsoft and affiliated companies.

Depending on the level of certification you achieve, you will qualify to display one of three logos on your business card and other personal promotional materials. These logos attest to the fact that you are proficient in the applications or cross-application skills necessary to achieve the certification.

Microsoft
Office Specialist

Microsoft
Office Specialist Expert

Microsoft
Office Specialist Master

Using the Logo Builder, you can create a personalized certification logo that includes the MOS logo and the specific programs in which you have achieved certification. If you achieve MOS certification in multiple programs, you can include multiple certifications in one logo.

For more information

To learn more about the Microsoft Office Specialist exams and related courseware, visit:

http://www.microsoft.com/learning/en/us/mos-certification.aspx

Microsoft Word 2013

This book covers the skills you need to have for certification as a Microsoft Office Specialist in Microsoft Word 2013. Specifically, you need to be able to complete tasks that demonstrate the following skill sets:

1 Create and manage documents

2 Format text, paragraphs, and sections

3 Create tables and lists

4 Apply references

5 Insert and format objects

With these skills, you can create, populate, format, and manage the types of documents most commonly used in a business environment.

Prerequisites

We assume that you have been working with Word 2013 for at least six months and that you know how to carry out fundamental tasks that are not specifically mentioned in the objectives for this Microsoft Office Specialist exam. Before you begin studying for this exam, you might want to make sure you are familiar with the information in this section.

Moving around in a document

You can view various parts of the active document by using the vertical and horizontal scroll bars. Using the scroll bars does not move the cursor—it changes only the part of the document displayed in the window. For example, if you drag the vertical scroll box down to the bottom of the scroll bar, the end of the document comes into view, but the cursor stays in its original location.

Here are some other ways to use the scroll bars:

- Click the up or down scroll arrow on the vertical scroll bar to move the document window up or down one line of text.
- Click above or below the scroll box to move up or down one screen.
- Click the left or right scroll arrow on the horizontal scroll bar to move the document window to the left or right several characters at a time.
- Click to the left or right of the scroll box to move left or right one screen.

You can also move around in a document by moving the cursor. You can click to place the cursor at a particular location, or you can press a key or a key combination to move the cursor.

The following table shows the keys and key combinations you can use to move the cursor quickly.

Pressing this key or combination	Moves the cursor
Left Arrow	Left one character at a time
Right Arrow	Right one character at a time
Down Arrow	Down one line at a time
Up Arrow	Up one line at a time
Ctrl+Left Arrow	Left one word at a time
Ctrl+Right Arrow	Right one word at a time
Home	To the beginning of the current line
End	To the end of the current line
Ctrl+Home	To the beginning of the document
Ctrl+End	To the end of the document
Ctrl+Page Up	To the beginning of the previous page
Ctrl+Page Down	To the beginning of the next page
Page Up	Up one screen
Page Down	Down one screen

Selecting text

Before you can edit or format text, you need to select it. You can select any amount of text by dragging through it. You can select specific units of text as follows:

- To select a word, double-click it. The word and the space following it are selected. Punctuation following a word is not selected.

- To select a sentence, click anywhere in the sentence while holding down the Ctrl key. The first character in the sentence through the space following the ending punctuation mark are selected.

- To select a paragraph, triple-click it. The paragraph and paragraph mark are selected.

You can select adjacent words, lines, or paragraphs by positioning the cursor at the beginning of the text you want to select, holding down the Shift key, and then pressing an arrow key or clicking at the end of the text that you want to select.

To select non-adjacent blocks of text, select the first block, hold down the Ctrl key, and then select the next block.

To select a block of text quickly, you can use the selection area—the empty area to the left of the document's text column. When the pointer is in the selection area, it changes from an I-beam to a right-pointing arrow. From the selection area, you can select specific units of text as follows:

- To select a line, click in the selection area to the left of the line.

- To select a paragraph, double-click in the selection area to the left of the paragraph.

- To select an entire document, triple-click anywhere in the selection area.

To deselect text, click anywhere in the document window except the selection area.

Applying basic formatting

You can change font attributes such as size, style, effects, color, and character spacing from the Font group on the Home tab, from the Mini Toolbar, and from the Font dialog box that opens when you click the Font dialog box launcher. You can also apply pre-defined text effects from the Text Effects And Typography menu that is available from the Font group.

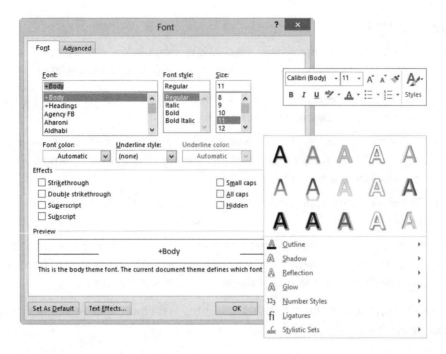

You can change paragraph attributes such as alignment, indentation, spacing, shading, and borders from the Paragraph group on the Home tab, and from the Paragraph dialog box that opens when you click the Paragraph dialog box launcher.

> **Strategy** Ensure that you are familiar with all the character and paragraph formatting options.

Cutting, copying, and pasting content

Word offers several different methods of cutting and copying content. After selecting the content, you can click buttons on the ribbon, use a keyboard shortcut, or right-click the selection and click commands on the shortcut menu. Cutting or copying content places it on the Microsoft Office Clipboard. You can paste content that is stored on the Clipboard into a document (or any Office file) by using commands from the ribbon, shortcut menu, or keyboard, or directly from the Clipboard. Experienced users might find it fastest to use a keyboard shortcut. The main keyboard shortcuts for editing tasks are shown in the following table.

Task	Keyboard shortcut
Cut	Ctrl+X
Copy	Ctrl+C
Paste	Ctrl+V
Undo	Ctrl+Z
Repeat/Redo	Ctrl+Y

When you paste content, Word gives you options for formatting the pasted content. Those options are available from the Paste Options menu that appears when you click the Paste arrow in the Clipboard group on the Home tab of the ribbon, or when you click the Paste Options button that appears below the lower-right corner of the pasted content.

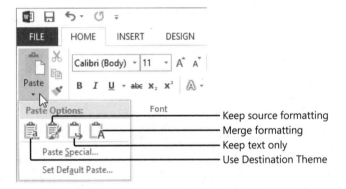

The available buttons depend on the format of the cut or copied selection (the source) and the format of the place you're pasting it (the destination). Pointing to a button displays a preview of how the source content will look if you use that option to paste it at the current location.

> **Tip** You can move or copy text by dragging it within the same document. To copy the selection instead of moving it, hold down the Ctrl key while you drag. The dragged text is not stored on the Clipboard, but the Paste Options list is available when you release the mouse button so that you can adjust the formatting of the moved or copied content.

> **See Also** For information about paste options, see section 2.1, "Insert text and paragraphs."

1 Create and manage documents

The skills tested in this section of the Microsoft Office Specialist exam for Microsoft Word 2013 relate to creating and managing documents. Specifically, the following objectives are associated with this set of skills:

1.1 Create documents

1.2 Navigate through documents

1.3 Format documents

1.4 Customize document options and views

1.5 Configure documents to print or save

You can create many types of documents in Word and modify the appearance and format to fit your needs.

This chapter guides you in studying ways of creating, working in, and saving documents; formatting the page size and content; printing documents; and modifying the Word program window to fit your needs.

> **Practice Files** To complete the practice tasks in this chapter, you need the practice files contained in the MOSWord2013\Objective1 practice file folder. For more information, see "Download the practice files" in this book's Introduction.

1.1 Create documents

Creating blank and custom documents from templates

When you start Word 2013 without opening an existing document, a Start screen appears. From this screen you can open a recent document or create a document—either a blank document based on the Normal template or a custom document based on another template. When Word is already running, you can create documents from the New page of the Backstage view.

Some templates are installed on your computer with Office, but you can download many others from the Office website. To locate a template suitable for your purposes, enter a search phrase in the Search Online Templates box and then click the Start Searching button, or click a category in the Suggested Searches list below the box.

The Start screen and New page display thumbnails of popular templates and templates that are specific to the season or an upcoming holiday. If you create custom templates and save them in your Personal Templates folder, Featured and Personal links appear below the search box. You can click these links to switch between viewing program-supplied templates and your own. If you save templates in a location other than your Personal Templates folder, you can create documents based on those templates either from File Explorer or from the Open page of the Backstage view.

> **Tip** In Windows 8, File Explorer has replaced Windows Explorer. Throughout this book, we refer to this utility by its Windows 8 name. If your computer is running Windows 7 or an earlier version of Windows, use Windows Explorer instead.

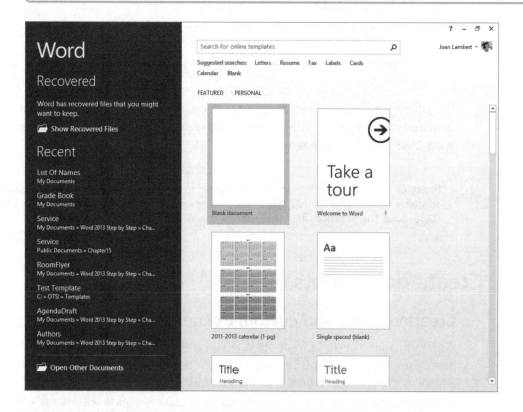

> **Tip** In Word 2013, you can choose your own Personal Templates folder from the Save page of the Word Options dialog box.

> **Strategy** The objective domain for Exam 77-418 includes coverage of creating documents based on existing templates. Creating and modifying document templates is part of the objective domain for Exam 77-419, Word 2013 Expert.

Clicking the thumbnail of a program-supplied template displays a preview and description of the document that will be created by the template, along with ratings provided by people who have downloaded the template.

➤ **To create a new blank document**

→ Start Word. When the program **Start** screen appears, do one of the following:

  ○ Press the **Esc** key.

  ○ Click the **Blank document** thumbnail.

→ Display the **New** page of the **Backstage** view, and then click the **Blank document** thumbnail.

➤ **To create a new document based on a custom template**

→ From the **Start** screen or from the **New** page of the **Backstage** view, locate the template from which you want to create a document, and then do one of the following:

  ○ Click the thumbnail, and then in the template information window, click **Create**.

  ○ Double-click the thumbnail.

→ In File Explorer, navigate to the template location and then double-click the template.

→ From the **Open** page of the **Backstage** view, navigate to the template location and then double-click the template.

Opening non-native files directly in Word

Word 2013 creates files in Office Open XML formats, which support a greater range of access and reuse options and produce a smaller file than earlier Word document formats. The default file format for a document created in Word 2013 is the .docx format, which supports all the Word 2013 features.

You can save Word 2013 files in these native file formats:

- **.docx** Word document

- **.docm** Word macro-enabled document

- **.dotx** Word document template

- **.dotm** Word macro-enabled document template

> **Tip** Although the file extensions are the same, Word 2013 recognizes a difference between files saved in Word 2013 and files of the same type saved in Word 2010 or Word 2007. A Word 2013 .docx file can be opened and edited in Word 2010 or Word 2007 on a computer running Windows, or in Word 2011 or Word 2008 on a Mac, but if it is saved in one of those programs, the next time you open it in Word 2013 it will be displayed in Compatibility View.

In addition to these native formats, Word 2013 supports many types of files that can be created in other programs, including the following:

- Files created in earlier versions of Word

- Files created in WordPerfect version 5 or 6

- OpenDocument Text files

- PDF files

- Plain Text files

- Rich Text Format files

- Webpages

- XML files

A particularly exciting feature of Word 2013 is the ability to edit PDF files in Word rather than in a third-party program such as Adobe Acrobat. You can open a PDF file in Word 2013 exactly as you would any other type of file. When you do so, Word converts the file to an editable Word document. If the file contains complicated formatting and layout, the Word version of the document might not be a perfect replica of the PDF file, but most simple files convert quite cleanly.

➤ **To open a non-native file in Word from File Explorer**

➔ Right-click the file, click **Open With**, and then click **Word (desktop)**.

➤ **To open a non-native file in Word from the program window**

1. On the **Open** page of the **Backstage** view, navigate to the file location.

2. In the **Open** dialog box, in the file type list to the right of the **File name** box, click **All Files** to display all the files in the folder, or click the specific type of file you want to locate.

3. In the **Open** dialog box, click the file you want to open, and then click **Open**.

Practice tasks

The practice files for these tasks are located in the MOSWord2013\Objective1 practice file folder. Save the results of the tasks in the same folder.

- Start Word. From the Start screen, create a new document based on the built-in Blank Document template. Save the document as *MyBlankDoc.docx*.

- In the open document, display the New page of the Backstage view. Locate the online template for a fax cover sheet that uses the Equity theme. Create a fax cover sheet based on this template. Save the document as *MyFaxCover.docx*.

- In File Explorer, navigate to the practice file folder. Create a document based on the *Word_1-1a* document template that is saved in that folder. Save the document as *MySummerDoc.docx*.

- In the open document, on the Open page of the Backstage view, navigate to the practice file folder. Display all text files in the folder, and then open the *Word_1-1b* text file in Word.

- From the practice file folder, open the *Word_1-1c* file in Word. Verify that you can modify the file content, and save the file as a new PDF document named *MyPDF.pdf*.

1.2 Navigate through documents

Searching for text

You can search for text from the Navigation pane or from the Find page of the Find And Replace dialog box. The Results page of the Navigation pane displays the search results in context, whereas the Find page locates only one instance of the search term at a time but allows you to define more search criteria.

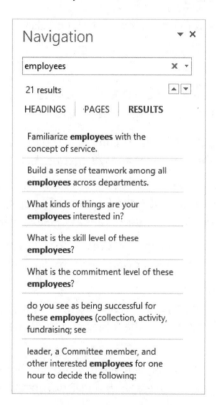

You can narrow the search results that are shown on the Results page of the Navigation pane by specifying search parameters. The parameters available for a Navigation pane search are limited, but usually sufficient for defining searches that don't include wild-cards, special characters, or formatting.

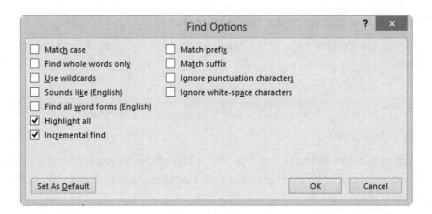

> **Tip** Selecting an option in the Find Options dialog box clears any current search results.

You can perform an even more specific search from the Find And Replace dialog box, in which you can specify many formatting options and also include special characters within your search term.

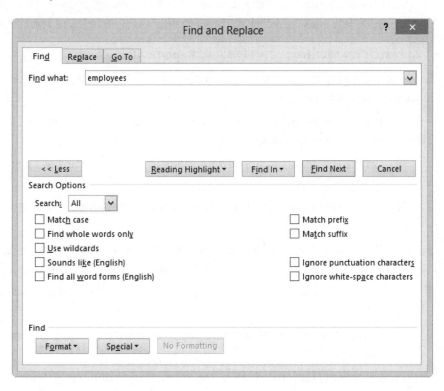

➤ **To search for text from the Navigation pane**

1. Display the **Results** page of the **Navigation** pane by using any of the following methods:

   ○ In the **Navigation** pane, click the **Results** link.

   ○ On the **Home** tab, in the **Editing** group, click the **Find** button.

   ○ Press **Ctrl+F**.

2. Enter characters in the search box at the top of the **Navigation** pane to highlight all occurrences of those characters in the document and display them on the **Results** page.

3. Scroll through the document to display the highlighted results or click any result in the **Navigation** pane to move directly to that occurrence.

4. Click the **Next** and **Previous** buttons to move among the results or to redisplay the results on the **Results** page.

➤ **To refine a Navigation pane search**

→ In the **Navigation** pane, click the **Search for more things** arrow at the right end of the search box, and then click **Options** to display a simple list of search options.

➤ **To search for text from the Find And Replace dialog box**

1. Display the **Find** page of the **Find and Replace** dialog box by using any of the following methods:

   ○ In the **Navigation** pane, click the **Search for more things** arrow at the right end of the search box, and then click **Advanced Find**.

   ○ On the **Home** tab, in the **Editing** group, click the **Find** arrow, and then click **Advanced Find**.

2. Click **More** in the lower-left corner of the dialog box to display additional search options.

3. In the **Find what** box, enter the text you want to search for, or click the **Special** button and then click the symbol or formatting symbol you want to locate.

4. Modify your search by selecting any of the following options in the expanded dialog box:

   ○ Guide the direction of the search by selecting **Down**, **Up**, or **All** from the **Search** list.

   ○ Locate only text that matches the capitalization of the search term by selecting the **Match case** check box.

- Exclude occurrences of the search term that appear within other words by selecting the **Find whole words only** check box.
- Find two similar words, such as *effect* and *affect*, by selecting the **Use wild-cards** check box and then including one or more wildcard characters in the search term.

> **Tip** The two most common wildcard characters are ?, which represents any single character in the given location, and *, which represents any number of characters in the given location. For a list of the available wildcards, select the Use Wildcards check box and then click the Special button.

- Find occurrences of the search text that sound the same but are spelled differently, such as *there* and *their*, by selecting the **Sounds like** check box.
- Find occurrences of a particular word in any form, such as *try*, *tries*, and *tried*, by selecting the **Find all word forms** check box.
- Locate formatting or styles by selecting them from the **Format** list.
- Locate words with the same beginning or end as the search term by selecting the **Match prefix** or **Match suffix** check box.
- Locate words with different hyphenation or spacing by selecting the **Ignore punctuation characters** or **Ignore white-space characters** check box.

Inserting hyperlinks

Word documents can include hyperlinks that provide a quick way to perform tasks such as the following:

- Link to a location within a document.
- Open another document.
- Link to a website.
- Download a file.
- Send an email message.

While creating a hyperlink to a document or a webpage, called the *target*, you can specify whether the target information should appear in the same window or frame as the active document or in a new one. You can also make a particular setting the default for all hyperlinks.

Within a document, hyperlinks appear underlined and in the color specified for hyperlinks by the document's theme. You can jump to the target of the hyperlink by holding down the Ctrl key and clicking the link. After you click the hyperlink, its color changes to the color specified for followed hyperlinks.

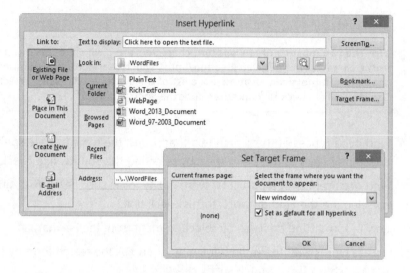

➤ **To insert a hyperlink to a file**

 1. Select the text or graphic object to which you want to attach the hyperlink.

> **Tip** You can change the selected text from within the Insert Hyperlink dialog box by changing it in the Text To Display box.

 2. Open the **Insert Hyperlink** dialog box by doing one of the following:

   ○ On the **Insert** tab, in the **Links** group, click the **Add a Hyperlink** button.

   ○ Right-click the selection, and then click **Hyperlink**.

   ○ Press **Ctrl+K**.

 3. In the **Insert Hyperlink** dialog box, on the **Link to** bar, click the **Existing File or Web Page** button.

 4. In the **Look in** area, browse to the target file.

   Or

   In the **Address** box, enter the absolute path to the target file.

 5. Click **Target Frame**. In the **Set Target Frame** dialog box, specify where the hyperlink target will be displayed, and then click **OK**.

 6. In the **Insert Hyperlink** dialog box, click **OK**.

➤ **To insert a hyperlink to a webpage**

1. Select the text or graphic object to which you want to attach the hyperlink, and then open the **Insert Hyperlink** dialog box.

2. On the **Link to** bar, click the **Existing File or Web Page** button.

3. In the **Address** box, enter the URL of the webpage or click the **Browsed Pages** button and select one from the list.

4. Click **Target Frame**. In the **Set Target Frame** dialog box, click **New window**, and then click **OK**.

5. In the **Insert Hyperlink** dialog box, click **OK**.

➤ **To insert a hyperlink to a heading or bookmark within the document**

1. Select the text or graphic object to which you want to attach the hyperlink, and then open the **Insert Hyperlink** dialog box.

2. On the **Link to** bar, click the **Place in This Document** button.

3. In the **Select a place in this document** box, click the heading or bookmark you want to link to.

4. In the **Insert Hyperlink** dialog box, click **OK**.

➤ **To insert a hyperlink that opens an email message form**

1. Select the text or graphic object to which you want to attach the hyperlink, and then open the **Insert Hyperlink** dialog box.

2. On the **Link to** bar, click the **E-mail Address** button.

3. In the **E-mail address** box, enter the email address to which you want to address the message.

   Or

   In the **Recently used e-mail addresses** list, click the email address to which you want to address the message.

4. In the **Subject** box, enter the subject of the message.

5. In the **Insert Hyperlink** dialog box, click **OK**.

➤ **To modify a hyperlink**

1. Right-click the hyperlink, and then click **Edit Hyperlink**.

2. In the **Edit Hyperlink** dialog box, make the necessary changes, and then click **OK**.

➤ **To remove a hyperlink**

→ Right-click the hyperlink, and then click **Remove Hyperlink**.

Creating bookmarks

Whether you are creating a document or working in a document created by someone else, you can insert named bookmarks to identify information to which you might want to return later. (Word automatically creates bookmark names for headings down to the fourth level by duplicating the heading; removing articles, spaces, and punctuation; and capitalizing the first letter of each word.) You can use whatever naming schema you like, provided it doesn't include spaces. You can move to bookmarked locations within a document either by creating hyperlinks to the bookmarks or by navigating to them.

> **Tip** Bookmarks are accessible in the Bookmark dialog box, on the Go To page of the Find And Replace dialog box, and in the Place In This Document list in the Insert Hyperlink dialog box.

> ➤ **To insert a bookmark**
>
> 1. Place the cursor at the location in which you want to insert the bookmark, or select the text or object to which you want to attach the bookmark.
>
> 2. On the **Insert** tab, in the **Links** group, click the **Bookmark** button.
>
> 3. In the **Bookmark** dialog box, enter a name for the bookmark in the **Bookmark name** box, and then click **Add**.

> **Tip** Bookmark names cannot contain spaces. If you include a space, the Add button becomes inactive. To name bookmarks with multiple words, either use internal capitalization or replace the spaces with underscores for readability.

➤ **To move to a bookmark**

1. Open the **Bookmark** dialog box, and then click the bookmark you want to move to.

2. Click **Go To**, and then click **Close**.

   Or

1. On the **Home** tab, in the **Editing** group, click **Go To** in the **Find** list.

2. On the **Go To** page of the **Find and Replace** dialog box, in the **Go to what** list, click **Bookmark**.

3. In the **Enter bookmark name** list, click the bookmark you want.

4. Click **Go To**, and then click **Close**.

Moving to specific locations and elements

From the Go To page of the Find And Replace dialog box, you can quickly move between pages, sections, lines, bookmarks, comments, footnotes, endnotes, fields, tables, graphics, equations, objects, or headings in a document.

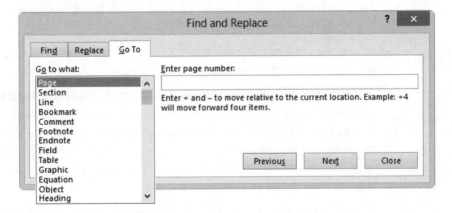

➤ **To use the Go To function to find elements within a document**

1. Display the **Go To** page of the **Find and Replace** dialog box by using one of the following methods:

   o On the **Home** tab, in the **Editing** group, click the **Find** arrow, and then click **Go To**.

   o Press **Ctrl+G**.

2. In the **Go to what** list, click the type of element you want to locate.

3. In the **Enter** *element* box, select or enter the identifier of the specific element you want to locate. Then click **Go To** to move to that element.

Or

Click the **Next** or **Previous** button to move among instances of the selected element in the document.

Practice tasks

The practice file for these tasks is located in the MOSWord2013\Objective1 practice file folder. Save the results of the tasks in the same folder.

- In the *Word_1-2* document, do the following:
  - ○ From the Results page of the Navigation pane, locate all instances of *to*. Then modify the search to locate all instances of *toy*. Move between the search results by using the navigation buttons.
  - ○ Modify your search to locate only instances of the capitalized word *Toymakers*.
  - ○ Perform an advanced search for all instances of *toy*, either capitalized or lowercase, that have the Heading 2 style applied.
  - ○ Locate the table of contents. Insert a hyperlink from each heading in the table of contents to the corresponding heading in the document.
  - ○ In the *Resources* section of the document, insert a hyperlink from the URL *www.wingtiptoys.com* to the corresponding website. Change the display text of the hyperlink from *www.wingtiptoys.com* to *the Wingtip Toys website* and ensure that the webpage will open in a new window. In the document, verify that clicking the hyperlink displays the Microsoft website home page in your default browser.
  - ○ In the *Contact Us* section of the document, insert a hyperlink from *sarah@wingtiptoys.com* that will create an email message addressed to you, with the subject *MOS Study Guide message*. Click the hyperlink to create the message, and then send the message to yourself.
  - ○ In the *Contact Us* section of the document, select the name *Lola Jacobsen* and insert a bookmark named *sales_manager*. Then attach a bookmark named *design_manager* to the name *Sarah Jones*.
  - ○ Return to the beginning of the document. Use the Go To function to move between graphics in the document, then to move to the top of page 3, and then to move to the *sales_manager* bookmark.

1.3 Format documents

Modifying page setup

You control the layout of the pages in a document. You can change the margins, orientation, and size of the document pages.

> **Tip** The document page size is unrelated to the paper size, which you set in the printer settings.

You can format text in multiple columns, and manually divide a document into pages or sections. When you define sections, you can set up the pages within an individual section differently from other pages of the document.

When appropriate to the document type, you can preface each line of text in the document with a line number. Line numbers can span the length of a document, restart at the beginning of each page or section, or skip text that you specify.

By default, Word breaks lines between words and after punctuation. When the automatic hyphenation feature is turned on, Word inserts line breaks and hyphens within words to help achieve a more uniform line length. You can stop Word from breaking a line between two words that you want to keep together by inserting a nonbreaking space between the words.

➤ **To change the page margins**

→ On the **Page Layout** tab, in the **Page Setup** group, click the **Margins** button, and then click the standard margin set you want.

Or

1. On the **Margins** menu, click **Custom Margins**.

2. On the **Margins** page of the **Page Setup** dialog box, specify the individual margins, the gutter width and position, the configuration of multiple pages, and the area of the document to which you want to apply the custom margins. Then click **OK**.

➤ **To change the page orientation**

→ On the **Page Layout** tab, in the **Page Setup** group, click the **Orientation** button, and then click **Landscape** or **Portrait**.

➤ **To change the page size**

→ On the **Page Layout** tab, in the **Page Setup** group, click the **Size** button, and then click the standard page size you want.

Or

1. On the **Size** menu, click **More Paper Sizes**.

2. On the **Paper** page of the **Page Setup** dialog box, select **Custom size** in the **Paper size** list, define the width and height of the page, and then click **OK**.

➤ **To format selected text into columns**

→ On the **Page Layout** tab, in the **Page Setup** group, click the **Columns** button, and then click the standard column configuration you want.

Or

1. On the **Columns** menu, click **More Columns**.

2. In the **Columns** dialog box, specify the number of columns, column width, and spacing, and then click **OK**.

➤ **To manually break column content**

→ Position the cursor where you want to insert the column break, and then do one of the following:

  ○ On the **Page Layout** tab, in the **Page Setup** group, click the **Breaks** button, and then in the **Page Breaks** group, click **Column**.

  ○ Press **Ctrl+Shift+Enter**.

➤ **To insert a manual page break**

→ Position the cursor where you want to insert the page break, and then do one of the following:

  ○ On the **Page Layout** tab, in the **Page Setup** group, click the **Breaks** button, and then in the **Page Breaks** group, click **Page**.

  ○ Press **Ctrl+Enter**.

➤ **To divide a document into sections**

1. Position the cursor at the beginning of the content with which you want to start the new section.

2. On the **Page Layout** tab, in the **Page Setup** group, click the **Breaks** button.

3. On the **Breaks** menu, in the **Section Breaks** group, click **Next Page**, **Continuous**, **Even Page**, or **Odd Page** to define the starting page of the new section.

➤ **To insert and control line numbers**

→ On the **Page Layout** tab, in the **Page Setup** group, click the **Line Numbers** button, and then click **Continuous**, **Restart Each Page**, **Restart Each Section**, or **Suppress for Current Paragraph**.

➤ **To automatically break lines and hyphenate words**

→ On the **Page Layout** tab, in the **Page Setup** group, click the **Hyphenation** button, and then click **Automatic**.

➤ **To control hyphenation settings**

1. On the **Page Layout** tab, in the **Page Setup** group, click the **Hyphenation** button, and then click **Hyphenation Options**.

2. In the **Hyphenation** dialog box, specify whether you want Word to automatically hyphenate the document or to hyphenate uppercase words, the maximum distance of a hyphen from the document margin (the hyphenation zone), and how many consecutive lines of a paragraph may be hyphenated. Then click **OK**.

➤ **To turn off automatic hyphenation**

→ On the **Page Layout** tab, in the **Page Setup** group, click the **Hyphenation** button, and then click **None**.

➤ **To selectively hyphenate words in a document**

1. On the **Page Layout** tab, in the **Page Setup** group, click the **Hyphenation** button, and then click **Manual**.

2. For each hyphenation suggested in the **Manual Hyphenation** dialog box, click **Yes** or **No**.

> **Tip** The No button is active only for existing hyphens.

➤ **To insert a nonbreaking space**

→ Press **Ctrl+Shift+Space**.

Or

1. On the **Insert** tab, in the **Symbols** group, click the **Symbol** button, and then click **More Symbols**.

2. On the **Special Characters** page of the **Symbol** dialog box, click **Nonbreaking Space**, and then click **Insert**.

Changing document themes

Every document you create is based on a template, and the appearance of the content within the template is controlled by a theme. The theme is a combination of coordinated colors, fonts, and effects that visually convey a certain tone. By default, Word applies the Office theme to all new, blank documents. To quickly change the appearance of a document, you can apply a different theme. To change the appearance of all new documents, you can make a different theme the default.

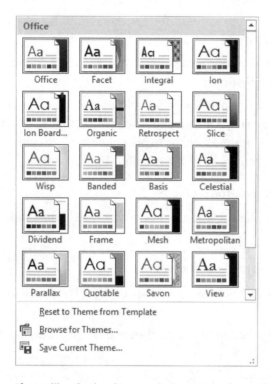

If you like the background elements of one theme but not the colors or fonts, you can mix and match theme elements. In addition to colors and fonts, you can control more subtle elements such as paragraph spacing and visual effects that are associated with a theme.

If you create a combination of theme elements that you would like to be able to use with other documents, you can save the combination as a new theme. When you save a theme in the default Document Themes folder, it is available in the Themes gallery.

You don't have to store custom themes in the Document Themes folder; you can store them anywhere on your hard disk, on removable media, or in a network location.

➤ **To apply a theme**

→ On the **Design** tab, in the **Document Formatting** group, click the **Themes** button, and then click the theme you want.

→ If the theme is stored outside of the default Document Themes folder, click **Browse for Themes** on the **Themes** menu, navigate to the theme you want, and then click **Open**.

➤ **To change the theme colors, fonts, paragraph spacing, or effects**

1. On the **Design** tab, in the **Document Formatting** group, click the **Theme Colors**, **Theme Fonts**, **Paragraph Spacing**, or **Theme Effects** button.

2. In the corresponding gallery, click the color scheme, font set, paragraph spacing, or combination of effects you want.

➤ **To save a modified theme**

1. Adjust the colors, fonts, or effects of the current theme to suit your needs.

2. In the **Themes** gallery, click **Save Current Theme**.

3. In the **Save Current Theme** dialog box, enter a name for the theme in the **File name** box, and then click **Save**.

➤ **To change the default theme**

1. Select the theme you want to use as the default, or modify the current theme.

2. On the **Design** tab, in the **Document Formatting** group, click **Set as Default**.

> **Strategy** The objective domain for Exam 77-418 includes coverage of applying existing themes, color schemes, font sets, paragraph spacing, and effects to documents. Creating those elements is part of the objective domain for Exam 77-419, Word 2013 Expert.

Changing document style sets

You can easily change the look of words, phrases, and paragraphs by using styles. More importantly, you can structure a document by applying paragraph styles that are linked to outline levels. In doing so, you build a document outline that is reflected in the Navigation pane and can be used to create a table of contents.

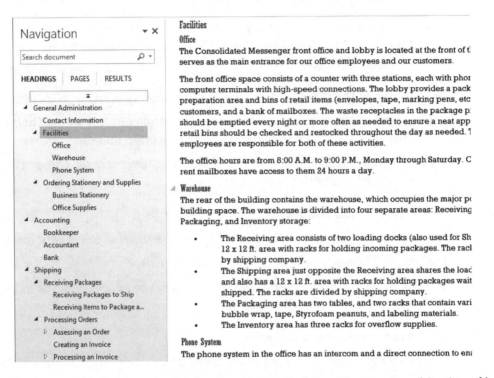

Styles can include character formatting, paragraph formatting, or a combination of both. Styles are stored in the template that is attached to a document. By default, blank new documents are based on the Normal template. The Normal template includes a standard selection of styles that fit the basic needs of most documents. These styles include nine heading levels, various text styles including those for multiple levels of bulleted and numbered lists, index and table of contents entry styles, and many specialized styles such as those for hyperlinks, quotations, placeholders, captions, and other elements. Commonly used styles are available in the Styles gallery on the Home tab.

You can access all the styles available in a document from the Styles pane, which you display by clicking the Styles dialog box launcher.

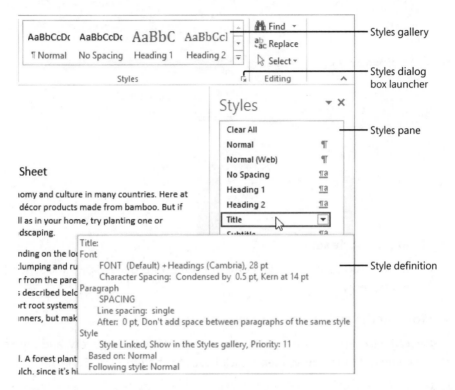

Styles stored in a template are usually based on the Normal style and use only the default body and heading fonts associated with the document's theme, so they all go together well. For this reason, formatting document content by using styles produces a harmonious effect. After you apply styles from the default style set, you can easily change the look of the entire document by switching to a different style set, which associates different formatting rules with the same styles. So if you have applied styles throughout a document, you can change the properties of the styles simply by changing the style set.

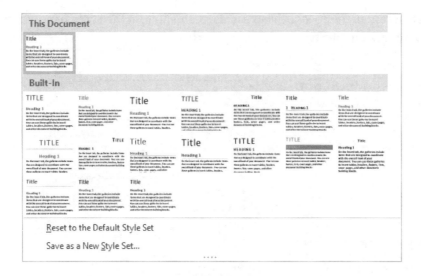

To apply a style set

→ On the **Design** tab, in the **Document Formatting** gallery, click the style set you want to apply.

To reset the style set to the template default

→ On the **Design** tab, expand the **Document Formatting** gallery, and then on the **Document Formatting** menu, click **Reset to the *template* Style Set**.

> **Strategy** The objective domain for Exam 77-418 includes coverage of applying existing style sets to documents. Creating and modifying custom style sets is part of the objective domain for Exam 77-419, Word 2013 Expert.

Inserting simple headers and footers

You can display information on every page of your document by creating headers and footers. You can populate and format headers and footers independently. You can have a different header and footer on the first page of a document, different headers and footers on odd and even pages, or different headers and footers for each section.

You can manually insert text or graphic elements in a header or footer, select common elements (such as page number, date and time, or a document property) from a menu, or insert a preformatted building block.

When the header or footer is active for editing, Word displays a dashed border between the header or footer and the document body, and the Design tool tab appears on the ribbon. You can enter information in the header and footer areas the same way you enter ordinary text. You can also use the commands on the Design tool tab to enter and format document information, move from one header or footer to another, and establish the location and position of the header and footer.

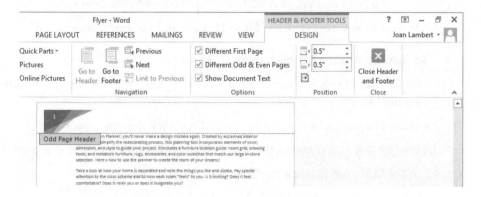

Tip If your document contains section breaks, each successive section inherits the headers and footers of the preceding section unless you break the link between the two sections. After you break the link, you can create a different header and footer for the current section.

You can manually insert a page number element in a header or footer, or you can use the separate Page Number feature to insert stylized page numbers.

See Also For more information about inserting preformatted page numbers, see "Inserting page numbers" later in this section. Word 2013 includes many preformatted header and footer building blocks. For information about building blocks, see section 5.1, "Insert and format building blocks."

> **To insert custom header or footer content**

1. Activate the header or footer by using one of these methods:

   ○ Position the cursor anywhere in the document. On the **Insert** tab, in the **Header & Footer** group, click the **Header** button or the **Footer** button, and then click the corresponding **Edit** command on the menu.

   ○ In Print Layout view, double-click in the top margin of a page to activate the header or in the bottom margin to activate the footer.

2. In the header or footer area, do any of the following:

○ Insert and format content by using the standard commands.

○ From the **Insert** group on the **Design** tool tab, insert the date, time, an image, document information, or any Quick Parts you want to include.

○ Use the preset tabs to align content at the left margin, in the center, and at the right margin, or modify the tabs to meet your needs.

3. In the **Close** group, click the **Close Header and Footer** button.

➤ **To insert a preformatted header or footer**

1. On the **Insert** tab, in the **Header & Footer** group, click the **Header** button or the **Footer** button.

2. In the **Header** gallery or the **Footer** gallery, click the design you want.

3. Replace any text placeholders and enter any other information you want to appear.

4. In the **Close** group, click the **Close Header and Footer** button.

➤ **To insert the current date and/or time in a header or footer**

1. In the header or footer, position the cursor where you want the date and/or time to appear.

2. On the **Design** tool tab, in the **Insert** group, click the **Insert Date and Time** button.

3. In the **Date and Time** dialog box, do the following, and then click **OK**:

○ Click the format in which you want the date and/or time to appear in the header or footer.

○ If you want Word to update the date and/or time in the header each time you save the document, select the **Update automatically** check box.

➤ **To modify standard header or footer settings**

1. On the **Design** tool tab, in the **Options** group, do any of the following:

○ Select the **Different First Page** check box if you want to use a different header or footer on the first page of the document. You might want to do this if, for example, the first page of the document is a cover page.

○ Select the **Different Odd & Even Pages** check box if you want to use different headers or footers for odd pages and for even pages. Select this option if the content of the header or footer is not centered and the document content will be viewed on facing pages.

○ Clear the **Show Document Text** check box if you find that you're distracted by the main document text when you're working in the header or footer.

2. In the **Position** group, set the **Header from Top** or **Footer from Bottom** distance.

3. In the **Close** group, click the **Close Header and Footer** button.

➤ **To delete a header or footer**

→ Activate the header or footer. Press **Ctrl+A** to select all the content of the header or footer, and then press **Delete**.

→ On the **Insert** tab, in the **Header & Footer** group, click **Header** or **Footer**, and then click the corresponding **Remove** command.

Inserting watermarks

A watermark is a transparent word or phrase, or a muted graphic, that appears on the page background of a document but doesn't interfere with its readability. You can use a text watermark such as *Draft* or *Important* to indicate information about a document. You can use a graphic watermark to brand a document with your logo or to simply add flair.

Watermarks are visible when you display a document in Print Layout view or Web Layout view, and are optional when printing a document.

About the Authors

Joan Lambert

Joan has worked in the training and certification industry for over 15 years. As President of OTSI, Joan is responsible for guiding the translation of technical information and requirements into useful, relevant, and measurable training and certification tools.

Joan is a Microsoft Certified Office Master, a Microsoft Certified Trainer (MCT), a Microsoft Certified Applications Specialist (MCAS) Instructor, a Microsoft Certified Technology Specialist (MCTS), and the author of more than two dozen books about Windows and Office (for Windows and Mac).

Joyce Cox

Joyce has over 30 years' experience in the development of training materials about technical subjects for non-technical audiences, and is the author of dozens of books about Office and Windows technologies. She is the Vice President of Online Training Solutions, Inc.

As President of and principal author for Online Press, she developed the Quick Course series of computer training books for beginning and intermediate adult learners. She was also the first managing editor of Microsoft Press, an editor for Sybex, and an editor for the University of California.

Online Training Solutions, Inc. (OTSI)

OTSI specializes in the design, creation, and production of Office and Windows training products for office and home computer users. For more information about OTSI, visit

www.otsi.com

➤ **To add a text watermark**

1. On the **Design** tab, in the **Page Background** group, click the **Watermark** button.

2. In the **Watermark** gallery, click the thumbnail for one of the predefined text watermarks.

    Or

1. On the **Watermark** menu, click **Custom Watermark**.

2. In the **Printed Watermark** dialog box, select **Text watermark**.

3. Either select the watermark text you want from the **Text** list, or enter the text in the **Text** box.

4. Format the text by changing the settings in the **Font**, **Size**, and **Color** boxes.

5. Choose a layout, select or clear the **Semitransparent** check box, and then click **OK**.

➤ **To use a picture as a watermark**

1. On the **Watermark** menu, click **Custom Watermark**.

2. In the **Printed Watermark** dialog box, select **Picture watermark**, and then click the **Select Picture** button.

3. In the **From a file** area of the **Insert Pictures** dialog box, click **Browse**. In the **Insert Picture** dialog box that opens, navigate to the folder where the picture is stored, and double-click the picture file to insert the file path in the **Printed Watermark** dialog box.

4. In the **Scale** list, choose how big or small you want the watermark picture to appear in the document.

5. If you want to display a more vibrant picture, clear the **Washout** check box. Then click **OK**.

Inserting page numbers

It is quite common to insert page numbers in a document that will be printed. You can insert stylized page numbers in the header, footer, left margin or right margin, or at the current cursor position on each page. You can format the page numbers to follow a specific pattern.

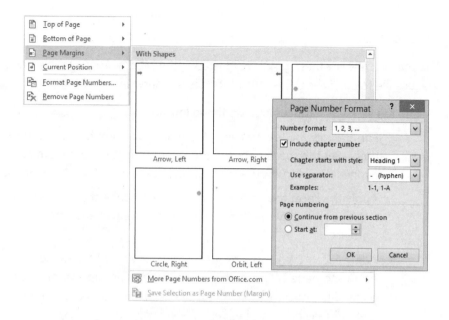

> ➤ **To insert a preformatted page number in a header or footer**

1. On the **Insert** tab, in the **Header & Footer** group, click the **Page Number** button.

2. In the **Page Number** list, click the location at which you want to insert the page number, and then click the page number style you want.

> ➤ **To change the format of page numbers**

1. On the **Insert** tab or **Design** tool tab (when the header or footer is active), in the **Header & Footer** group, click the **Page Number** button, and then click **Format Page Numbers**.

2. In the **Page Number Format** dialog box, in the **Number format** list, click the format you want.

3. Select any other options you want, and then click **OK**.

Practice tasks

The practice files for these tasks are located in the MOSWord2013\Objective1 practice file folder. Save the results of the tasks in the same folder.

- In the *Word_1-3a* document, do the following:
  - ○ Format only the text between the empty paragraph marks in three columns. Set the space between the columns to *0.3"*. Turn on automatic hyphenation and ensure that consecutive lines will not be hyphenated.
  - ○ Apply the Facet theme to the document. Change the theme colors to those specified by the Red Orange palette, and change the font set to Corbel.
  - ○ Add a Facet (Even Page) header to page 2, and a Facet (Odd Page) header to page 3. Ensure that a header does not appear on the first page of the document, and that the even and odd pages of the document display different headers.
  - ○ Add a diagonal text watermark that displays the phrase *Example Only* to the page background. Format the text of the watermark as semitransparent 54-point orange text. Verify that the watermark appears on all pages of the document.
- Modify the appearance of the *Word_1-3b* document by applying the Casual style set. Add page numbers that use the Circle, Right page number style in the right margin of the document. Then format the page numbers as uppercase Roman numerals.

1.4 Customize document options and views

Changing document views

In Word, you can display a document in a variety of views, each suited to a specific purpose.

The document views available in Word 2013 include the following:

- **Print Layout view** This view displays a document on the screen the way it will look when printed. You can review elements such as margins, page breaks, headers and footers, and watermarks.

- **Read Mode view** This view displays as much of the content of the document as will fit on the screen at a size that is comfortable for reading. In this view, the ribbon is replaced by one toolbar at the top of the screen with buttons for searching and navigating in the document. You can view existing comments, but you can't make changes to the document while in this view.

- **Web Layout view** This view displays the document the way it will look when viewed in a web browser. You can review backgrounds and other effects. You can also review how text wraps to fit the window and how graphics are positioned.

- **Outline view** This view displays the structure of a document as nested levels of headings and body text, and provides tools for viewing and changing the hierarchy.

- **Draft view** This view displays the content of a document with a simplified layout so that you can quickly enter and edit text. You cannot view layout elements such as headers and footers.

The View Shortcuts toolbar includes buttons for changing the view of the document window.

View Shortcuts toolbar

➤ **To switch views**

→ On the **View** tab, in the **Views** group, click the **Read Mode**, **Print Layout**, **Web Layout**, **Outline View**, or **Draft View** button.

→ At the right end of the status bar, on the **View Shortcuts** toolbar, click the **Read Mode**, **Print Layout**, or **Web Layout** button.

Changing magnification levels

You can adjust the magnification of a document by using the tools available in the Zoom group on the View tab, or the Zoom slider or Zoom Level button at the right end of the status bar.

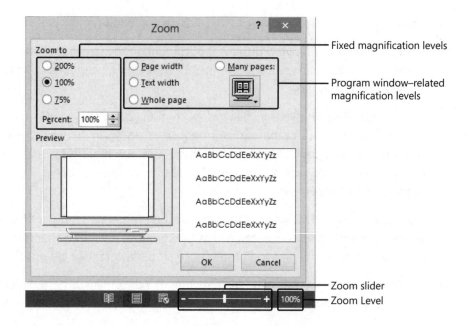

Fixed magnification levels

Program window–related magnification levels

Zoom slider
Zoom Level

➤ **To zoom in or out in 10-percent increments**

→ Click the **Zoom In** (+) button or the **Zoom Out** (-) button.

➤ **To zoom to a specific magnification**

→ Drag the **Zoom** slider.

→ On the **View** tab, in the **Zoom** group, click the **100%** button.

Or

1. Do either of the following:

  ○ Click the **Zoom level** button.

  ○ On the **View** tab, in the **Zoom** group, click the **Zoom** button.

2. In the **Zoom** dialog box, click a fixed magnification level, or in the **Percent** box, enter or select a magnification level. Then click **OK**.

➤ **To zoom to a program window–related magnification**

→ In the **Zoom** dialog box, do one of the following, and then click **OK**:

  ○ Click **Page width**, **Text width**, or **Whole page**.

  ○ Click **Many pages**, click the monitor icon below the option, and then click the page configuration you want (from 1x1 to 2x4 pages).

→ On the **View** tab, in the **Zoom** group, click the **One Page**, **Multiple Pages**, or **Page Width** button.

Customizing the Quick Access Toolbar

By default, buttons representing the Save, Undo, and Redo commands appear on the Quick Access Toolbar. If you regularly use a few commands that are scattered on various tabs of the ribbon and you don't want to switch between tabs to access the commands, you can add them to the Quick Access Toolbar so that they're always available to you. You can add commands to the Quick Access Toolbar from the Customize Quick Access Toolbar menu (which includes 11 common commands), from the ribbon, or from the Word Options dialog box. You can add any type of command to the Quick Access Toolbar, even a drop-down list of options or gallery of thumbnails.

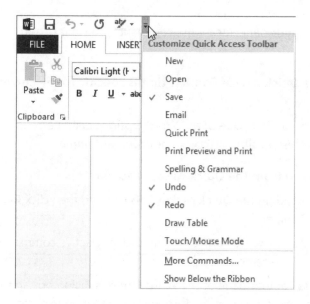

The default Quick Access Toolbar appears in all Word documents. You can also create a separate Quick Access Toolbar that is embedded in a specific document.

As you add commands to the Quick Access Toolbar, it expands to accommodate them. If you add a lot of commands, it might become difficult to view the text in the title bar, or some commands on the Quick Access Toolbar might be hidden. To resolve this problem, you can move the Quick Access Toolbar below the ribbon.

> ➤ **To change the location of the Quick Access Toolbar**

  ➜ On the **Customize Quick Access Toolbar** menu, click **Show Below the Ribbon** or **Show Above the Ribbon**.

  ➜ Right-click the **Quick Access Toolbar**, and then click **Show Quick Access Toolbar Below the Ribbon** or **Show Quick Access Toolbar Above the Ribbon**.

  ➜ On the **Quick Access Toolbar** page of the **Word Options** dialog box, select or clear the **Show Quick Access Toolbar below the Ribbon** check box.

➤ **To add a command to the Quick Access Toolbar**

→ At the right end of the **Quick Access Toolbar**, click the **Customize Quick Access Toolbar** button (the arrow), and then click one of the common commands displayed on the menu.

→ Right-click a command on the ribbon, and then click **Add to Quick Access Toolbar**.

Or

1. Display the **Quick Access Toolbar** page of the **Word Options** dialog box.

2. In the **Choose commands from** list, click the group of commands from which you want to select.

3. In the **Choose commands** pane, locate the command you want to add. Then click the **Add** button.

➤ **To create a separate Quick Access Toolbar that is specific to the current document**

→ On the **Quick Access Toolbar** page of the **Word Options** dialog box, in the **Customize Quick Access Toolbar** list, click **For *document name***.

➤ **To remove a command from the Quick Access Toolbar**

→ Right-click the command on the **Quick Access Toolbar**, and then click **Remove from Quick Access Toolbar**.

→ On the **Customize Quick Access Toolbar** menu, click any active command (indicated by a check mark) to remove it.

→ On the **Quick Access Toolbar** page of the **Word Options** dialog box, in the **Quick Access Toolbar** pane, click the command. Then click the **Remove** button.

➤ **To change the order of commands on the Quick Access Toolbar**

→ On the **Quick Access Toolbar** page of the **Word Options** dialog box, in the **Quick Access Toolbar** pane, click a command you want to move. Then click the **Move Up** or **Move Down** button.

➤ **To separate commands on the Quick Access Toolbar**

→ On the **Quick Access Toolbar** page of the **Word Options** dialog box, in the **Quick Access Toolbar** pane, click the command after which you want to insert a separator. At the top of the **Choose commands** pane, click **<Separator>**. Then click **Add**.

➤ **To reset the Quick Access Toolbar to its default content**

→ On the **Quick Access Toolbar** page of the **Word Options** dialog box, click the **Reset** button, and then click **Reset only Quick Access Toolbar** or **Reset all customizations**.

Customizing the ribbon

Experienced users who upgrade to Word 2013 might identify a few commands that no longer seem to be available. Lesser-used commands do not appear on the ribbon; instead, they are hidden in dialog boxes or panes, or not available at all from the standard user interface. You can make any of these commands easily accessible by adding it to the Quick Access Toolbar or to the ribbon.

➤ **To display a list of commands that do not appear on the ribbon**

→ On the **Quick Access Toolbar** or **Customize Ribbon** page of the **Word Options** dialog box, in the **Choose commands from** list, click **Commands Not in the Ribbon**.

➤ **To modify the ribbon tabs and groups**

1. Display the **Customize Ribbon** page of the **Word Options** dialog box.

2. In the **Customize the Ribbon** list, click the group of tabs on which you want to modify content.

3. In the **Customize the Ribbon** pane, do any of the following:

    ○ To prevent a tab from appearing on the ribbon, clear the check box that precedes the tab name.

    ○ To allow a tab to appear on the ribbon, select the check box that precedes the tab name.

    ○ To remove a group from a tab, click the **Expand** button that precedes the tab name to display its groups, then click a group name and click the **Remove** button.

    > **Tip** The group is not removed from the program, only from the tab.

    ○ To change the display name of a built-in tab or group, click the tab name or group name, and then click the **Rename** button. In the **Rename** dialog box, enter the name you want in the **Display name** box, and then click **OK**.

    ○ To move a group of commands to another tab, expand the source and destination tabs, and click the group you want to move. Then drag the group to its new location or click the **Move Up** or **Move Down** button until the group is where you want it.

➤ **To add a tab to the ribbon**

1. Select the tab after which you want the new tab to appear, and then click the **New Tab** button.

2. Click **New Tab (Custom)**, and then click the **Rename** button.

3. In the **Rename** dialog box, enter the name you want to assign to the custom tab in the **Display name** box, and then click **OK**.

➤ **To add a group to a tab**

1. Select the tab on which you want the group to appear, and then click the **New Group** button.

2. Click **New Group (Custom)**, and then click the **Rename** button.

3. In the **Rename** dialog box, click the icon that you want to appear when the custom group is condensed. In the **Display name** box, enter the name you want to assign to the custom group. Then click **OK**.

➤ **To add a command to a custom group**

1. On the **Customize Ribbon** page of the **Word Options** dialog box, in the **Customize the Ribbon** pane, click the custom group to which you want to add the command.

2. In the **Choose commands from** list, click the group of commands from which you want to select.

3. In the **Choose commands** pane, locate the command you want to add, and then click the **Add** button.

> **Tip** You can add commands to and remove commands from custom groups but not predefined groups.

➤ **To remove a command from a custom group**

→ On the **Customize Ribbon** page of the **Word Options** dialog box, in the **Customize the Ribbon** pane, click the command. Then click the **Remove** button.

➤ **To reset the ribbon to its default content and configuration**

→ On the **Customize Ribbon** page of the **Word Options** dialog box, click the **Reset** button, and then click **Reset only selected Ribbon tab** or **Reset all customizations**.

Splitting the window

It can be cumbersome to work in a long document that requires you to frequently scroll up and down to view data elsewhere in the document.

In any view other than Read Mode, you can display multiple parts of a document at one time by splitting the window. You can then independently scroll and work in two views of the document within one program window. The Navigation pane and any active panes are displayed for the entire document, as part of the program window. Each part of the split window has its own ruler and scroll bars. Some commands (such as the Zoom commands and some views) apply only to the currently active part of the split window; others apply to the currently selected content or to the entire document.

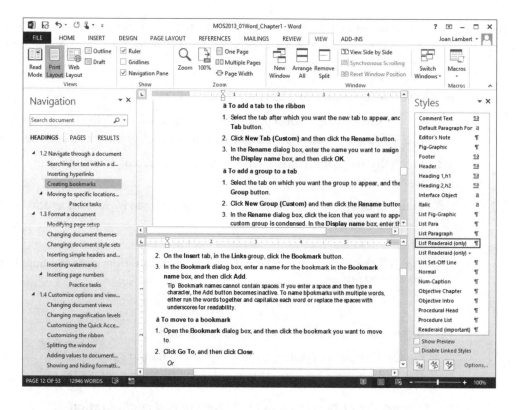

> ### To split the window
>
> → On the **View** tab, in the **Window** group, click the **Split** button.

Tip You can change the program window area allocated to each split pane by dragging the split bar up or down.

> ### To remove a split
>
> → Double-click the split bar that divides the panes.
>
> → Drag the split bar to the top of the scroll bar.
>
> → On the **View** tab, in the **Window** group, click the **Remove Split** button.

Modifying document properties

In Word 2013, the properties of a document are easily accessible from the Info page of the Backstage view. You can view and modify some properties directly on the Info page, or you can work in the Document Panel or Properties dialog box.

Properties ˅

Size	30.5KB
Pages	2
Words	822
Total Editing Time	95 Minutes
Title	Simple Room Design
Tags	information sheet; inf...
Comments	Finalize before distribu...

Related Dates

Last Modified	Today, 6:30 PM
Created	10/30/2012 10:18 PM
Last Printed	

Related People

Author Joyce Cox

 Joan Lambert

Add an author

Last Modified By Joan Lambert

Related Documents

📄 Open File Location

Show All Properties

> ### To set or change the Title, Tags, or Comments properties

→ On the **Info** page of the **Backstage** view, click the property to activate it, and then add or change information.

> ### To add an author to the Author property

→ On the **Info** page of the **Backstage** view, in the **Related People** area, click **Add an author**, and then do one of the following:

  ○ Enter one or more author names or email addresses, separated by semicolons, and then click **Verify the contact names you have entered** to validate the entry against your organization's Global Address List and your other Microsoft Outlook address books.

> **Tip** If Word finds a match for the author's name and you have his or her contact information stored in Outlook, you can initiate contact with that person from the Author list on the Info page.

○ Click the **Search the Address Book for contacts** button. In the **Address Book** dialog box, select the address book in which the author's contact information is saved, and then select the author.

➤ **To remove an author from the Author property**

→ On the **Info** page of the **Backstage** view, in the **Related People** area, right-click the author, and then click **Remove Person**.

➤ **To display the Document Panel**

→ On the **Info** page of the **Backstage** view, click **Properties**, and then click **Show Document Panel**.

➤ **To display the Properties dialog box**

→ On the **Info** page of the **Backstage** view, click **Properties**, and then click **Advanced Properties**.

→ In File Explorer, right-click the file, and then click **Properties**.

Showing and hiding formatting symbols

When you are fine-tuning the layout of a document, you might find it helpful to display formatting marks and hidden characters. Formatting marks, such as tabs, paragraph marks, page breaks, and section breaks, control the layout of your document, and hidden characters provide the structure for behind-the-scenes processes, such as indexing.

➤ **To display or hide formatting marks and hidden characters**

→ On the **Home** tab, in the **Paragraph** group, click the **Show/Hide ¶** button.

→ Press **Ctrl+Shift+8 (Ctrl+*)**.

Recording simple macros

Macros are useful for completing repetitive tasks or tasks that you perform frequently. You can record a series of simple actions that you perform in Word and save the recorded actions as a macro. If you want to automate a more advanced task and have some basic coding skills, you can record the basic actions and then modify the code in the recorded macro to meet your needs.

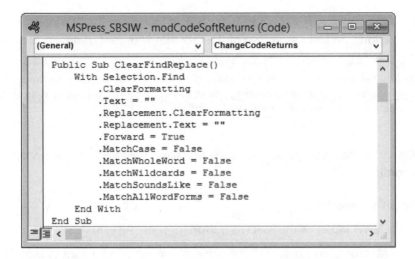

```
MSPress_SBSIW - modCodeSoftReturns (Code)

(General)                          ChangeCodeReturns

Public Sub ClearFindReplace()
    With Selection.Find
        .ClearFormatting
        .Text = ""
        .Replacement.ClearFormatting
        .Replacement.Text = ""
        .Forward = True
        .MatchCase = False
        .MatchWholeWord = False
        .MatchWildcards = False
        .MatchSoundsLike = False
        .MatchAllWordForms = False
    End With
End Sub
```

➤ **To record a macro**

1. On the **View** tab, click the **Macros** arrow, and then click **Record Macro**.

2. In the **Record Macro** dialog box, enter a name for the macro in the **Macro name** box. The name cannot include spaces.

3. In the **Store macro in** list, click the template or document in which you want to save the macro.

4. If you want to assign the macro to a button on the Quick Access Toolbar, do the following:

   a. In the **Assign macro to** area, click **Button**.

   b. On the **Quick Access Toolbar** page of the **Word Options** dialog box, click the macro name in the left pane, click **Add**, and then click **Modify**.

   c. In the **Modify Button** dialog box, select a symbol to display on the button. Then click **OK** in each of the open dialog boxes.

5. If you want to assign the macro to a keyboard shortcut, do the following:

   a. In the **Assign macro to** area, click **Keyboard**.

   b. In the **Customize Keyboard** dialog box, with the cursor in the **Press new shortcut key** box, press the key combination you want to assign to the macro. If the shortcut is already assigned to another macro, or to a symbol or command, the existing target is shown below the **Current keys** box.

   c. After verifying that you want to assign the selected keyboard shortcut, click **Assign**, and then click **Close**.

6. When the cursor shape changes to a cassette to indicate that Word is recording your actions, perform each step of the task that you want to record as a macro.

> **Tip** You can perform the task by clicking commands or by pressing buttons. If you want to select text, do so by clicking the keyboard buttons and not by dragging the mouse; the macro engine doesn't record mouse selections.

7. When you complete the task, click the **Macros** arrow, and then click **Stop Recording**.

➤ **To modify a macro**

1. On the **View** tab, click the **Macros** button (or press **Alt+F8**).

2. In the **Macros** dialog box, click the name of the macro you want to modify, and then click **Edit**.

3. In the **Microsoft Visual Basic for Applications** window, select the macro you want to modify, and then edit the code.

Assigning keyboard shortcuts

You can use keyboard shortcuts to run commands, insert symbols, and run macros. Many commands and symbols already have associated keyboard shortcuts. The keyboard shortcut for a command that appears on the ribbon is displayed by default in the ScreenTip that appears when you point to the command. If a command you use frequently doesn't have a built-in keyboard shortcut, or if you don't like the keyboard shortcut that is assigned to the command, you can create one either in a specific document or in a template. You can also modify the built-in keyboard shortcuts.

➤ **To manage keyboard shortcuts for commands**

1. Display the **Customize Ribbon** page of the **Word Options** dialog box.

2. Below the **Choose commands** pane, to the right of **Keyboard shortcuts**, click the **Customize** button.

3. In the **Customize Keyboard** dialog box, select the category containing the command for which you want to create a keyboard shortcut, and then select the command.

> **Tip** The Current Keys box displays any keyboard shortcut already assigned to the command.

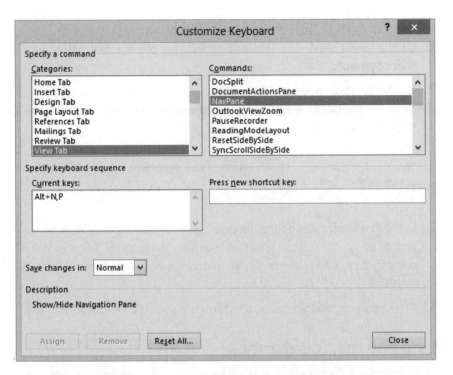

4. Click to position the cursor in the **Press new shortcut key** box, and then press the key combination you want to use as a keyboard shortcut for the selected command.

> **Tip** In the area below the Current Keys box, Word indicates whether the keyboard shortcut is currently assigned to a command or unassigned.

5. To delete an existing keyboard shortcut to make it available for reassignment, select it in the **Current keys** box, and then click the **Remove** button.

6. To assign an available keyboard shortcut to the selected command, do one of the following:

   ○ To save the keyboard shortcut in all documents based on the current template, verify that the template name is selected in the **Save changes in** list, and then click **Assign**.

   ○ To save the keyboard shortcut only in the current document, click the document name in the **Save changes in** list, and then click **Assign**.

7. To delete all custom keyboard shortcuts, click **Reset All**.

8. Close the **Customize Keyboard** dialog box and the **Word Options** dialog box.

➤ **To assign a keyboard shortcut to a symbol**

1. On the **Insert** tab, in the **Symbols** group, click the **Symbol** button, and then click **More Symbols**.

2. On the **Symbols** page of the **Symbol** dialog box, locate and click (don't double-click) the symbol to which you want to assign a shortcut key, and then click the **Shortcut Key** button.

> **Tip** If a shortcut key has been assigned to the symbol, it is shown in the lower-right corner of the Symbols page.

3. In the **Customize Keyboard** dialog box, press the key combination you want to assign to the symbol. If the shortcut is already assigned to another symbol, or to a command or macro, the target symbol or command is shown below the **Current keys** box.

4. After verifying that you want to assign the selected keyboard shortcut, click **Assign**.

Managing macro security

When you open a document that contains macros, the macros are automatically disabled, and an information bar alerts you to that fact. You can work in the document without enabling the macros, but if you want to use a macro, you must first enable them.

➤ **To enable macros in an open document**

→ On the **Message Bar**, click **Enable Content**.

→ On the **Info** page of the **Backstage** view, click the **Enable Content** button, and then do one of the following:

○ Click **Enable All Content**.

○ Click **Advanced Options**. In the **Microsoft Office Security Options** dialog box, click **Enable content for this session**, and then click **OK**.

Practice tasks

The practice files for these tasks are located in the MOSWord2013\Objective1 practice file folder. Save the results of the tasks in the same folder.

- Open the *Word_1-4a* document, and then do the following:
    - Display the document content in Read Mode view, in narrow columns.
    - Display two pages of the document side by side in Print Layout view.
    - Split the window, and display the document view in the upper split pane at 235% and the document view in the lower split pane at 45%. Then close the lower split pane and display the document at page width.
    - Add the Format Painter button, the Shading button, and the Styles gallery from the Home tab to a Quick Access Toolbar that appears only in this document. Then add the Insert A Comment button, the Track Changes button, and the Compare button from the Review tab, and separate them from the previously added commands.
    - Display the Developer tab on the ribbon and hide the Mailings tab. Create a custom tab named *Favorites*. Move the Proofing group of commands from the Review tab to the Favorites tab. Create a custom group named *Colors* on the Favorites tab. Add the Text Highlight Color, Font Color, and Shading buttons to the Colors group.
- In the *Word_1-4b* document, do the following:
    - Set the Title property to *All About Bamboo* and the Subject property to *bamboo*.
    - Assign the keywords *rhizomes*, *tropical*, and *mites* to the document.
    - Add yourself as the only author.
    - Add a custom Document Number property, and set it to *1001*.
- In the *Word_1-4c* document, create a macro named *BoldColor* that starts at the beginning of the document, locates the phrase *Microsoft Office Specialist*, and formats the selected phrase as bold, red text. Save the macro only in the current document, and add a button that runs the macro to the Quick Access Toolbar. Position the insertion point at the beginning of the third paragraph of the document, and then run the macro from the Quick Access Toolbar.
- After successfully completing the practice tasks, reset the Quick Access Toolbar and ribbon to their default configurations.

1.5 Configure documents to print or save

Configuring documents to print

When printing a document, you can specify what part of the document is printed and whether markup (tracked changes) is indicated in the printed document. In addition, you have the option of printing the following information instead of the document content:

- Document properties
- Tracked changes
- Styles
- AutoText entries
- Custom shortcut keys

In addition to these options, you can specify the following print settings:

- Print a multipage document on one or both sides of the paper. If your printer supports double-sided printing, you have the option of flipping the double-sided page on the long edge or the short edge (depending on how you plan to bind and turn the document pages).

> **Important** Some of the settings on the Print page of the Backstage view are dependent on the functionality supported by your printer. These settings may vary when you select a different device in the Printer list.

- Print multiple copies of a document either with collated pages (all pages of each copy together) or uncollated pages (all copies of each page together).
- Print up to 16 pages on each sheet of paper. You can use this option to print a booklet with two pages per sheet that will be folded in the middle. You might also use this option to save paper when you're printing a long document, but bear in mind that as the number of pages per sheet increases, the size of the content printed on the page decreases.
- If your printer has multiple paper trays or a manual paper feeder, select the paper source you want to use.

➤ **To select a printer**

→ On the **Print** page of the **Backstage** view, in the **Printer** area, click the current printer, and then click the printer you want to use.

Print

Copies: 1

Print

Printer ⓘ

HP LaserJet
Ready

Printer Properties

Settings

Print All Pages
The whole thing

Pages: ⓘ

Print One Sided
Only print on one side of th...

Collated
1,2,3 1,2,3 1,2,3

Landscape Orientation

Letter
8.5" x 11"

Mirrored Margins
Inside: 2" Outside: 1"

1 Page Per Sheet

Page Setup

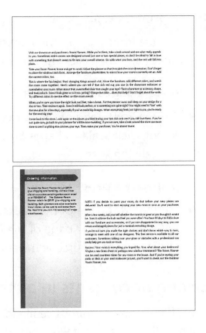

➤ **To print multiple copies of a document**

→ On the **Print** page of the **Backstage** view, in the **Copies** box, click the arrows or enter the number of copies you want to print. If you want to print the copies of each page separately, click **Collated** in the **Settings** area, and then click **Uncollated**.

➤ **To print a specific portion of a document**

→ On the **Print** page of the **Backstage** view, in the **Settings** area, click **Print All Pages** and then do any of the following:

  ○ To print only the currently selected content, click **Print Selection**.

  ○ To print only the page on which the cursor is active, click **Print Current Page**.

  ○ To print specific pages or sections, click **Custom Print** and enter the pages, sections, or page ranges you want to print in the **Pages** box. Indicate page ranges by using a hyphen and multiple page selections by using a comma (for example, *1-3, 6* prints pages 1, 2, 3, and 6). Indicate sections and page ranges within sections by prefacing the page with *p* and the section with *s* (for example, *s2* prints the entire second section, and *p2s2-p4s2* prints pages 2-4 of the second section).

➤ **To print a document double-sided**

→ On the **Print** page of the **Backstage** view, in the **Settings** area, click **Print One Sided** and then click the **Print on Both Sides** option that you want.

➤ **To print multiple pages on each sheet of paper**

→ On the **Print** page of the **Backstage** view, in the **Settings** area, click **1 Page per Sheet** and then click the number of pages you want to print on each sheet.

➤ **To scale pages to a specific size**

→ On the **Print** page of the **Backstage** view, in the **Settings** area, click **1 Page per Sheet**, click **Scale to Paper Size**, and then click the paper size to which you want to scale the sheets.

➤ **To specify a paper source**

→ On the **Print** page of the **Backstage** view, in the **Settings** area, click the **Page Setup** link. On the **Paper** page of the **Page Setup** dialog box, in the **Paper source** area, click the paper source you want. Then click **OK**.

Saving documents in alternate file formats

The Office 2013 programs use file formats based on XML, called the *Microsoft Office Open XML Formats*, that were introduced with Office 2007. By default, Word 2013 files are saved in the .docx format, which is the Word variation of this file format. The .docx format provides the following benefits:

- File size is smaller because files are compressed when saved, decreasing the amount of disk space needed to store the file and the amount of bandwidth needed to send files in email, over a network, or across the Internet.

- Recovering at least some of the content of damaged files is possible because XML files can be opened in a text program such as Notepad.

- Security is greater because .docx files cannot contain macros, and personal data can be detected and removed from the file. (Word 2013, Word 2010, and Word 2007 provide a different file format—.docm—for documents that contain macros.)

In addition to these default Word 2013 formats, you can save a document that you create in Word 2013 in many other formats, including Word Macro-Enabled Document, Word Macro-Enabled Template, Word XML Document, Web Page, Word 97-2003 Template, Word 2003 XML Document, Strict Open XML Document, and Works 6-9 Document.

If you want to save a Word document in a format that can be opened by the widest variety of programs (including text editors that are installed with most operating systems), use one of these two formats:

- **Rich Text Format (.rtf)** This format preserves the document's formatting.

- **Plain Text (.txt)** This format preserves only the document's text.

If you want people to be able to view a document exactly as it appears on your screen, use one of these two formats:

- **PDF (.pdf)** This format is preferred by commercial printing facilities. Recipients can display the file in the free Microsoft Reader or Adobe Reader programs, and can display and edit the file in Word 2013 or Adobe Acrobat.

- **XPS (.xps)** This format precisely renders all fonts, images, and colors. Recipients can display the file in the free Microsoft Reader program or the free XPS Viewer program.

The PDF and XPS formats are designed to deliver documents as electronic representations of the way they appear when printed. Both types of files can easily be sent by email to many recipients and can be made available on a webpage for downloading by anyone who wants them. However, the files are no longer Word documents. A PDF file can be converted to the editable Word format. An XPS file cannot be opened, viewed, or edited in Word.

When you save a Word document in PDF or XPS format, you can optimize the file size of the document for your intended distribution method—the larger Standard file size is better for printing, whereas the Minimum file size is suitable for online publishing. You can also configure the following options:

- Specify the pages to include in the PDF or XPS file.
- Include or exclude comments and tracked changes in a PDF file.
- Include or exclude non-printing elements such as bookmarks and properties.
- Select compliance, font embedding, and encryption options in a PDF file.

➤ **To save a file in an alternative file format with the default settings**

→ In the **Save As** dialog box, in the **Save as type** list, click the format you want.

→ On the **Export** page of the **Backstage** view, click **Change File Type** and then click the file type you want.

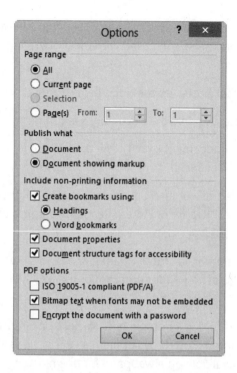

> ➤ **To save a file in PDF or XPS format with custom settings**

1. On the **Export** page of the **Backstage** view, click **Create PDF/XPS Document**, and then click the **Create PDF/XPS** button.

2. In the **Publish As PDF or XPS** dialog box, click **Options**.

3. In the **Options** dialog box, select the options you want for the PDF or XPS file, and then click **OK**.

   Or

1. Display the **Save As** dialog box. In the **Save as type** list, click either **PDF** or **XPS Document**.

2. In the **Save As** dialog box, click **Options**.

3. In the **Options** dialog box, select the options you want for the PDF or XPS file, and then click **OK**.

Maintaining backward compatibility

If you work with people who are using a version of Word earlier than 2007, they can install the free Microsoft Office Compatibility Pack For Word, Excel, And PowerPoint File Formats from the Microsoft Download Center at *download.microsoft.com*. The

Compatibility Pack doesn't provide additional functionality in the older program version, but it does enable users to open .docx files in the older version of Word.

To ensure that the appearance and functionality of a document is consistent in current and earlier versions of Word, you can run the Compatibility Checker. This tool identifies formatting and features that aren't supported or won't work as expected in earlier versions of Word.

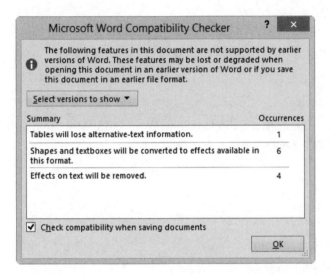

The following Word 2013 formatting and features aren't supported in Word 2003 or earlier versions of Word:

- Word 2007 content controls
- Themes
- Major/minor fonts
- Tracked moves
- Margin tabs
- SmartArt graphics
- Office 2007 charts
- Open XML Embedded objects
- Building blocks
- Bibliographies and citations
- Equations
- Relative text boxes

In addition to those previously listed, the following Word 2013 formatting and features aren't supported by Word 2007 or earlier versions of Word:

- New numbering formats
- New shapes and text boxes
- Text effects
- Alt text for tables
- OpenType features
- Blocking authors
- New WordArt effects
- New content controls

In addition to those previously listed, the following Word 2013 formatting and features aren't supported by Word 2010 or earlier versions of Word:

- Web video
- Apps for Office
- Repeating section content controls
- Customized footnote columns
- Collapsed by Default headings
- Marking comments as done

➤ **To run the Compatibility Checker before saving a document**

1. On the **Info** page of the **Backstage** view, click the **Check for Issues** button, and then click **Check Compatibility**.

2. In the **Select versions to show** list, select the Word versions you want to support, and clear the Word versions against which you do not want to validate the document. Selected versions are indicated by check marks preceding the version.

➤ **To maintain backward compatibility with a previous version of Word**

1. When saving the document, choose the previous file format in the **Save as type** list.

2. In the **Microsoft Word Compatibility Checker** window, click **Continue** to convert the unsupported features.

Saving files to remote locations

From the Save As page of the Backstage view, you can connect to a variety of storage locations, including a Microsoft OneDrive, Microsoft SharePoint site, or other online storage location; a folder on your computer; or another network location. The locations available from the Save As page vary depending on where you have previously saved files.

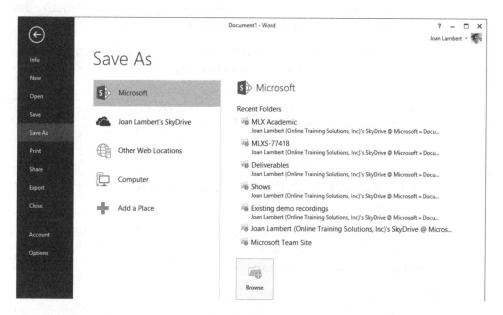

> ➤ **To add a SharePoint site that is not associated with Office 365 to your Web Locations list**

1. On the **Save As** page of the **Backstage** view, click **Other Web Locations**, and then click **Browse**.

2. In the **Save As** dialog box, enter the URL of the SharePoint site in the **Address** bar, and then click the **Go to** button.

3. Enter your user credentials for the SharePoint site, and then click **OK**.

> ➤ **To add an Office 365 SharePoint site or OneDrive to your Save As locations**

1. On the **Save As** page of the **Backstage** view, click **Add a Place**.

2. In the **Add a Place** list, click **Office 365 SharePoint** or **OneDrive**.

3. In the **Add a service** window, enter the email address with which you sign in to the SharePoint site or OneDrive, and then click **Next**.

4. In the **Sign In** window, enter your user credentials for the SharePoint site or OneDrive, and then click **Sign in**.

➤ **To save a document to a remote location**

1. On the **Save As** page of the **Backstage** view, click the type of remote location in which you want to save the file.

2. In the remote location list, click the folder in which you want to save the file, or click **Browse** and then enter your credentials for the remote location.

3. In the **Save As** dialog box, navigate to an existing folder or create a new folder, modify the name in the **File name** box if necessary, and then click **Save**.

> **Tip** You can share a file with other people while saving it to a shared remote location by selecting options on the Share page of the Backstage view.

Protecting documents by using passwords

Sometimes, you might want only certain people to be able to open and change a document. The easiest way to exercise this control is to assign a password to protect the document. Word then requires that the password be entered correctly before it will allow the document to be opened and changed.

Word offers two levels of password protection:

- **Unencrypted** The document is saved in such a way that only people who know the password can open it, make changes, and save the file. People who don't know the password can open a read-only version. If they make changes and want to save them, they have to save the document with a different name or in a different location, preserving the original.

- **Encrypted** The document is saved in such a way that people who do not know the password cannot open it at all.

➤ **To require a password to modify a document**

1. On the **Save As** page of the **Backstage** view, click **Browse**. Then enter or select a save location and file name for the password-protected document, if necessary.

> **Tip** Save the password-protected document in the original location to overwrite the current version, or in another location to retain the unprotected original.

4. In the **Confirm Password** dialog box, enter the password in the **Reenter password to modify** box, and then click **OK**.

5. In the **Save As** dialog box, click **Save**. If prompted to do so, click **Yes** to confirm that you want to replace the existing file.

> **To require a password to open a document**

1. On the **Info** page of the **Backstage** view, click the **Protect Document** button, and then click **Encrypt with Password**.

2. In the **Encrypt Document** dialog box, enter the password you want to assign to the document in the **Password** box, and then click **OK**.

   Or

1. On the **Save As** page of the **Backstage** view, click **Browse**. Then enter or select a save location and file name for the password-protected document, if necessary.

2. In the **Save As** dialog box, click **Tools**, and then click **General Options**.

3. In the **General Options** dialog box, in the **Password to open** box, enter the password you want to assign to the document. Then click **OK**.

Tip Instead of setting a password, you can select the Read-Only Recommended check box to cause Word to display a message suggesting that the document be opened as read-only.

---

4. In the **Confirm Password** dialog box, in the **Reenter password to open** box, enter the password, and then click **OK**.

5. In the **Save As** dialog box, click **Save**. If prompted to do so, click **Yes** to confirm that you want to replace the existing file.

> **To remove unencrypted password protection**

1. On the **Save As** page of the **Backstage** view, click **Browse**. Then enter or select a save location and file name for the password-protected document, if necessary.

2. In the **Save As** dialog box, click **Tools**, and then click **General Options**.

3. In the **General Options** dialog box, delete the contents of the **Password to open** or **Password to modify** box. Then click **OK**.

4. In the **Save As** dialog box, click **Save**. Then click **Yes** to confirm that you want to replace the existing file.

➤ **To remove encrypted password protection**

1. Open the document by using the password.

2. On the **Info** page of the **Backstage** view, in the **Protect Document** list, click **Encrypt with Password**.

3. In the **Encrypt** dialog box, delete the contents of the **Password** box, and then click **OK**.

Practice tasks

The practice files for these tasks are located in the MOSWord2013\Objective1 practice file folder. Save the results of the tasks in the same folder.

- Open the *Word_1-5a* document, and do the following:

  - Print only the first section of the document, with two pages on each sheet of paper.

  - Assign an encrypted password that permits a person to open a read-only or read/write copy of the document. Close the document, and open a read-only copy. Then remove the password protection.

- Open the *Word_1-5b* document. Save a copy of the file as a PDF file named *MyPDF* that is optimized for online presentation and includes bookmarks to all the document headings. Then open the *MyPDF* file in a PDF reading pro-gram (such as Microsoft Reader), display the bookmarks, and ensure that you can move to specific headings by clicking the bookmarks.

- Open the *Word_1-5c* document and review its content. Save a copy of the document named *MyCompatible* that is compatible with Word 2002. Then open the copy in Word 2013, ensure that *Compatibility Mode* appears in the title bar, and review any changes.

Objective review

Before finishing this chapter, ensure that you have mastered the following skills:

1.1 Create documents

1.2 Navigate through documents

1.3 Format documents

1.4 Customize document options and views

1.5 Configure documents to print or save

2 Format text, paragraphs, and sections

The skills tested in this section of the Microsoft Office Specialist exam for Microsoft Word 2013 relate to formatting document content. Specifically, the following objectives are associated with this set of skills:

2.1 Insert text and paragraphs

2.2 Format text and paragraphs

2.3 Order and group text and paragraphs

Word documents are merely containers for their content. The way that you present that content—by formatting its appearance and structure and by maintaining consistency—can improve the effectiveness of the document in communicating a specific message.

This chapter guides you in studying ways of inserting text, symbols, special characters, document properties, and fields by using different methods; formatting text and creating WordArt objects; formatting paragraph indentation, spacing, and layout; and structuring a document by inserting page and section breaks.

> **Practice Files** To complete the practice tasks in this chapter, you need the practice files contained in the MOSWord2013\Objective2 practice file folder. For more information, see "Download the practice files" in this book's Introduction.

2.1 Insert text and paragraphs

> **See Also** For basic information about cutting, copying, and pasting content, see the "Prerequisites" section that precedes the objective coverage.

Pasting and appending text

Cutting, copying, pasting, and moving text are basic skills within Microsoft Office programs. The Microsoft Office Clipboard stores items (up to 24) that have been cut or copied from any Office program. When the Clipboard is full, the oldest item is deleted when a new one is added. All items are deleted when you turn off the computer, or you can manually delete individual items or all items.

Invoking the Paste command pastes the newest item from the Clipboard. You can view and work with all the items that have been cut or copied to the Clipboard in the Clipboard pane.

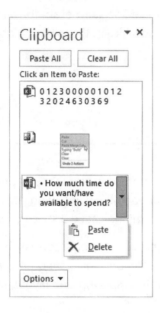

> ➤ **To manage the display of the Clipboard pane**

→ To manually display the Clipboard, on the **Home** tab, click the **Clipboard** dialog box launcher.

→ To control the automatic display of the Clipboard, click **Options** at the bottom of the **Clipboard** pane, and then select one of the following:

    ○ To always display the Clipboard when you cut or copy an item, select **Show Office Clipboard Automatically**.

    ○ To display the Clipboard only when you use a specific keyboard shortcut, select **Show Office Clipboard When Ctrl+C Pressed Twice**.

    ○ To never display the Clipboard automatically, select **Collect Without Showing Office Clipboard**.

→ To close the Clipboard pane, click the **Close** button at the right end of its title bar.

> ➤ **To manage items in the Clipboard pane**

  → To paste an individual item at the cursor, click the item; or point to the item, click
     the arrow that appears, and then click **Paste**.

  → To paste all the items stored on the Clipboard at the same location, click the **Paste
     All** button.

  → To remove an item from the Clipboard, point to the item, click the arrow that
     appears, and then click **Delete**.

  → To remove all items from the Clipboard, click the **Clear All** button.

Items are pasted from the Clipboard with the default formatting specified in the Cut,
Copy, And Paste section of the Advanced page of the Word Options dialog box. You
can change the default behavior to suit your needs, select a paste option from the Paste
menu in the Clipboard group, or paste an item and then select a paste option from the
shortcut menu. Available paste options vary based on the source content and destination formatting, and can be related to any type of formatting applied to the content.

> **Tip** By default, the Use Smart Cut And Paste check box is selected on the Advanced page
> of the Word Options dialog box, so Word inserts and deletes any necessary spaces. To
> control the spacing yourself, clear this check box.

> ➤ **To override the default formatting when pasting content**

  → Paste the content by using a standard method, click the **Paste Options** button that
     appears near the lower-right corner of the pasted content, and then select the
     paste option you want.

  → On the **Home** tab, in the **Clipboard** group, click the **Paste** arrow, and then in the
     Paste Options section of the menu, click the option you want.

Pasting content in alternative formats

You can paste cut or copied content into a document in a variety of formats by clicking
Paste Special on the Paste menu. If you cut or copy a file, Microsoft PowerPoint slide,
or other individual item, options to paste a linked copy of the item or of a representa-
tive icon are active. When you paste a link, you can update the linked item if the original
item changes. And you can paste a hyperlink to the copied item so that you can easily
jump to the original from the linked copy.

The Paste Special dialog box lists formats that are valid for the content that was most
recently placed on the Clipboard. These might include such formats as Picture, Bitmap,
Device Independent Bitmap, GIF, PNG, JPEG, Formatted Text, Unformatted Text,
Unformatted Unicode Text, HTML, Word Document Object, Excel Worksheet Object,
PowerPoint Slide Object, and Files.

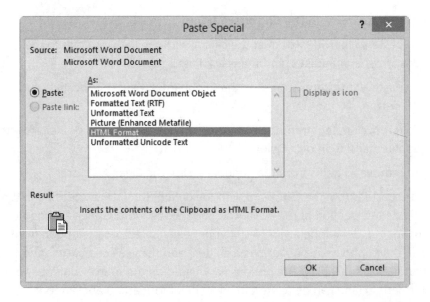

➤ **To paste a cut or copied item or content in a different format**

1. On the **Home** tab, in the **Clipboard** group, click the **Paste** arrow, and then click **Paste Special**.

2. In the **Paste Special** dialog box, click the format you want, and then click **OK**.

➤ **To paste a link or hyperlink to a copied item**

1. In the **Paste Special** dialog box, click **Paste link**, and then click the format you want.

2. To display an icon rather than the item content, select the **Display as icon** check box.

3. Click **OK**.

➤ **To update a linked copy to reflect changes to the original**

➜ Right-click the copy, and then click **Update Link**.

Appending text to documents

You can quickly append the contents of other documents to the active document without having to copy and paste large quantities of content or content from multiple sources.

➤ **To append content to the current document**

1. Press **Ctrl+End** to position the cursor at the end of the document. Ensure that the cursor is in a blank paragraph.

2. On the **Insert** tab, in the **Text** group, click the **Object** arrow (not the button), and then click **Text from File**.

3. In the **Insert File** dialog box, browse to and select the document or documents you want to insert. Then click the **Insert** button.

Finding and replacing text

When developing document content, you can ensure that the text in your documents is consistent and accurate by using the Find feature to review every occurrence of a specific word or phrase, or the Replace feature to consistently modify text, formatting, or styles.

You can conduct simple text searches from the Navigation pane. You can conduct more complex searches, and replace search terms with other text or special characters, from the Find And Replace dialog box.

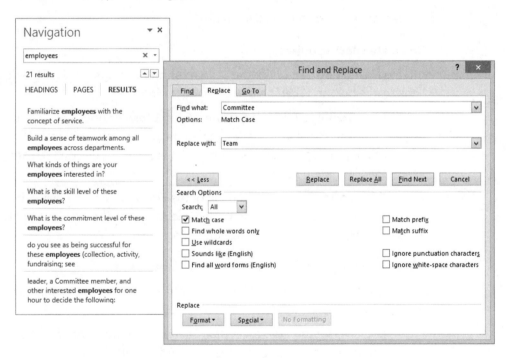

➤ **To locate specific text**

1. In the **Navigation** pane, enter the text in the **Search** box.

> **Tip** Press Ctrl+F to place the cursor in the Navigation pane search box.

2. Display the **Results** page of the **Navigation** pane, and then do any of the following:

- ○ Point to a search result to display the number of the page on which it appears and the heading that precedes it.

- ○ Click a search result to display it in the document.

- ○ Click the **Previous** or **Next** button to move among the search results.

- ○ Click the **End your search** button (the X) at the right end of the search box to clear the search results.

➤ **To restrict text search results from the Navigation pane**

1. In the **Navigation** pane, click the **Search for more things** arrow at the right end of the search box, and then click **Options**.

2. In the **Find Options** dialog box, select the search criteria you want, and then click **OK**.

3. Enter the search text in the **Search** box.

➤ **To locate specific objects**

→ In the **Navigation** pane, click the **Search for more things** arrow at the right end of the search box, and then do one of the following:

- ○ Click **Graphics**, **Tables**, **Equations**, **Footnotes/Endnotes**, or **Comments** to highlight all instances of the item in the document and on the Headings page of the Navigation pane, and display the specific results on the Pages page of the Navigation pane.

- ○ Click **Go To**. On the **Go To** page of the **Find and Replace** dialog box, click the type of object you want to locate, and then click the **Previous** or **Next** button to move among those items in the document.

➤ **To locate nonspecific text and special characters**

1. Display the **Find** page of the **Find and Replace** dialog box by doing any of the following:

- ○ In the **Navigation** pane, click the **Search for more things** arrow at the right end of the search box, and then click **Advanced Find**.

- ○ On the **Home** tab, in the **Editing** group, in the **Find** list, click **Advanced Find**.

2. With the cursor in the **Find what** box, click **Any character**, **Any digit**, or **Any letter**, or click the special character you want to locate.

3. Enter any text fragments or formatting that accompany the text or character you want to locate, and then click **Find Next**:

> ➤ **To locate and replace text**

1. Display the **Replace** page of the **Find and Replace** dialog box by doing any of the following:

  ○ In the **Navigation** pane, click the **Search for more things** arrow at the right end of the search box, and then click **Replace**.

  ○ On the **Home** tab, in the **Editing** group, click **Replace**.

  ○ Press **Ctrl+H**.

2. In the **Find what** box, specify the text or characters you want to locate.

3. In the **Search Options** area, select the check boxes of any applicable search options.

> **Tip** The settings in the Search Options area apply to the search term and not to the replacement term.

4. In the **Replace with** box, enter the text or characters with which you want to replace the search term.

> **Tip** You can't specify wildcard characters in the Replace With box. You can specify special characters. For example, you can use the Replace feature to remove blank paragraph marks from a document by replacing ^p^p (two paragraph marks) with ^p (one paragraph mark).

5. Do any of the following:

  ○ Click **Find Next** to find the next occurrence of the search term.

  ○ Click **Replace** to replace the selected occurrence with the text in the **Replace with** box and move to the next occurrence.

  ○ Click **Replace All** to replace all occurrences of the search term in the document without individually reviewing them.

> **Tip** You can quickly review all instances of a search term by searching from the Navigation pane and then scrolling through them on the Results page.

Inserting symbols and special characters

Some documents require characters not found on a standard keyboard. These characters might include the copyright (©) or registered trademark (®) symbols, currency symbols (such as € or £), Greek letters, or letters with accent marks. Or you might want to add arrows (such as ↗ or ↘) or graphic icons (such as ☎ or ✈). Word gives you easy access to a huge array of symbols that you can easily insert into any document. Like graphics, symbols can add visual information or eye appeal to a document. However, they are different from graphics in that they are actually characters associated with a specific font.

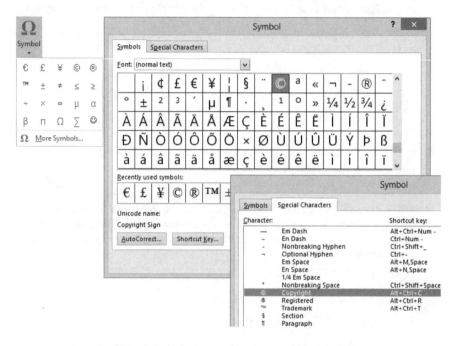

> **Tip** You can insert some common symbols by using a keyboard shortcut. You can review the assigned keyboard shortcuts in the Symbol dialog box and the AutoCorrect Options dialog box.

➤ To insert a common symbol

→ On the **Insert** tab, in the **Symbols** group, click the **Symbol** button, and then click the symbol you want to insert.

→ Enter any of the following keyboard shortcuts:

  ○ To insert a copyright symbol, enter *(c)* or press **Alt+Ctrl+C**.

  ○ To insert a Euro symbol, enter *(e)*.

  ○ To insert a registered trademark symbol, enter *(r)* or press **Alt+Ctrl+R**.

  ○ To insert a trademark symbol, enter *(tm)* or press **Alt+Ctrl+T**.

> **Tip** If you turn off the Replace Text As You Type option in the AutoCorrect settings, the parenthetical code will not convert to the symbol.

➤ **To insert a special character**

1. On the **Insert** tab, in the **Symbols** group, click the **Symbol** button, and then click **More Symbols**.

2. On the **Special Characters** page of the **Symbol** dialog box, double-click the character you want to insert.

Or

On the **Symbols** page of the **Symbol** dialog box, locate and double-click the symbol you want to insert.

> **Tip** The dialog box might be positioned in front of the cursor.

3. After you insert all the symbols you want, close the **Symbol** dialog box.

Inserting text and symbols by using AutoCorrect

The AutoCorrect feature corrects common spelling errors and capitalization issues. AutoCorrect includes a default list of frequently misspelled words and their correct spellings. It also includes text shortcuts for commonly used symbols.

In addition to using it for its standard purpose, you can use the AutoCorrect feature to insert text that you frequently enter in documents. Rather than entering an entire phrase, you can enter an abbreviation that isn't a standard word, and have AutoCorrect replace it for you. For example, you could create the text shortcut *tyfyb* for the phrase *Thank you for your business*.

➤ **To add a text shortcut to the AutoCorrect list**

1. On the **Proofing** page of the **Word Options** dialog box, click **AutoCorrect Options**.

2. On the **AutoCorrect** page of the **AutoCorrect** dialog box, enter the text shortcut you want to use in the **Replace** box.

> **Tip** If you enter and select the text shortcut in the document before displaying the AutoCorrect dialog box, the Replace box will be prefilled with the text shortcut.

3. Enter the text with which you want AutoCorrect to replace the text shortcut in the **With** box. Click **Add**, and then click **OK**.

> **Strategy** The objective domain for Exam 77-418, "Microsoft Word 2013," includes using the AutoCorrect feature to insert text. You can also use the AutoText function to insert text or formatted content in a document. The use of AutoText and other Quick Parts is part of the objective domain for Exam 77-419, "Microsoft Word 2013 Expert."

Inserting properties and fields

Section 1.4, "Customize document options and views," includes saving information as document properties. You can insert document properties into a document—for example, on a title page or in a header or footer—as a field. If you edit the field contents in the document or the property value from the Backstage view, the change is reflected in the other location.

Fields are other values that are defined and saved with a document. You can insert a field that tells Word to supply specified information or to perform a specified action in a specified way. Inserting a field in a document displays the field value. The field code that generates the value consists of a set of curly braces containing the field name and any required or optional instructions or settings. These settings, called *switches*, refine the results of the field—for example, by formatting it in a particular way. Different fields have different field options—some have only general options, whereas others have multiple types of switches. You can't enter field codes directly in a document; you must insert them from the Field dialog box.

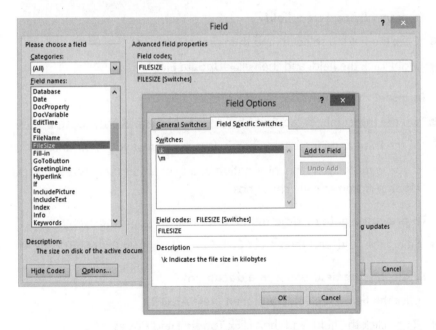

Inserting some types of fields requires advanced knowledge of the fields and how to control them. However, some fields are very easy. For example, several fields in the Date And Time category provide useful information. By default, date and time fields are updated every time you open the document.

➤ **To insert a dynamic document property**

→ On the **Insert** tab, in the **Text** group, click the **Quick Parts** button, click **Document Property**, and then click the property you want to insert.

➤ **To insert a field**

1. On the **Insert** tab, in the **Text** group, click the **Quick Parts** button, and then click **Field**.

2. In the **Field** dialog box, do the following, and then click **OK**:

   a. In the **Field names** list, click the field you want to insert.

   b. In the **Field properties** or **Advanced field properties** area, set any properties associated with the field.

   c. To display or hide the field syntax, click **Field Codes** or **Hide Codes**.

   d. To add optional switches, click **Options**. In the **Field Options** dialog box, click any switch you want to add, and click **Add to Field**. Then click **OK**.

➤ **To manually update a field**

→ Click the field to select it, and then press **F9**.

→ Right-click the field, and then click **Update Field**.

➤ **To insert the current date and time**

1. On the **Insert** tab, in the **Text** group, click the **Date & Time** button.

2. In the **Date and Time** dialog box, select the format you want to use.

3. If you want to insert the information as a field rather than as regular text, select the **Update Automatically** check box.

➤ **To prevent a date or time field from updating automatically**

→ Select the field, and then press **Ctrl+F11** to lock it (or **Ctrl+Shift+F11** to unlock it).

➤ **To display the field codes in a document**

→ Click the field to select it, and then press **Alt+F9**.

→ Right-click the field, and then click **Toggle Field Codes**.

Practice tasks

The practice files for these tasks are located in the MOSWord2013\Objective2 practice file folder. Save the results of the tasks in the same folder.

- Open the *Word_2-1a* document and do the following:
  - ○ In the first paragraph, insert the registered trademark symbol (®) after the word *Microsoft*.
  - ○ Replace all instances of *(trademark)* in the document with the trademark symbol (™). Ensure that you replace only instances in which the word *trademark* is in parentheses, and no other version of the word.
  - ○ Save the document, but don't close it.
- Open the *Word_2-1b* presentation in PowerPoint. In the left pane, click the Slide 2 thumbnail. Use any technique to copy the slide to the Clipboard.
- Return to the *Word_2-1a* document and do the following:
  - ○ Display the Clipboard pane and verify that the copied slide is the most recent item on the Clipboard.
  - ○ In the blank second paragraph, paste a linked copy of Slide 2 in place of the text *<link to slide here>*.
  - ○ In the document header, replace the word *Title* with the Title document property and set the property to *All About Word*. Then after *Last Saved:*, insert the date and time that the document was most recently saved, in the format *m/dd/yyyy h:mm:ss* and ensure that they will update each time the document is saved.
  - ○ Save the document, but don't close it.
- In the *Word_2-1b* presentation, with Slide 2 active, click the slide header and change *Design* to *Design Features*. Then on the Quick Access Toolbar, click the Save button.
- Return to the *Word_2-1a* document and do the following:
  - ○ Verify that the document displays the most recent version of the linked slide.
  - ○ Update the save date and ensure that it reflects the most recent save.
  - ○ Append the contents of the *Word_2-1c* document to the end of the *Word_2-1a* document.
- Save and close the open files.

2.2 Format text and paragraphs

Formatting text by using the Replace command

In addition to searching for words and phrases in the Find And Replace dialog box, you can use the dialog box to search for a specific character format, paragraph format, or style, and replace it with a different one. By using this method, you can locate specific words or content types and apply character or paragraph styles to that content.

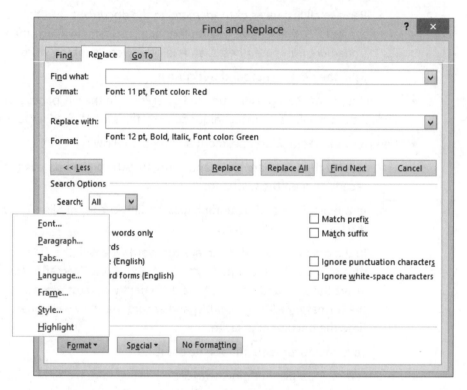

➤ **To replace a specific format with a different format**

1. On the **Home** tab, in the **Editing** group, click the **Replace** button.

   Or

   Press **Ctrl+H**.

2. On the **Replace** page of the **Find and Replace** dialog box, click the **More** button to expand the dialog box if it isn't already expanded.

3. In the **Find what** box, enter the text you want to locate, if applicable.

> **Tip** Searching for a format without specifying text locates all instances of that format.

4. In the **Replace** section, on the **Format** menu, click **Font**, **Paragraph**, **Tabs**, **Language**, **Frame**, **Style**, or **Highlight**. In the dialog box corresponding to your menu selection, indicate the format or style you want to find, and then click **OK**.

5. Click in the **Replace with** text box and enter the replacement text, if applicable. On the **Format** menu, click the format category with which you want to replace the original formatting. In the corresponding dialog box, indicate the replacement format or style, and then click **OK**.

6. Click **Find Next** to locate the first occurrence of the specified format, and then click **Replace** to replace that one occurrence or **Replace All** to replace every occurrence.

Formatting text by using Format Painter

Format Painter is a convenient tool that you can use to copy formatting from one location to another. When using Format Painter you have the option of copying the formatting to one location or to multiple locations.

➤ **To copy existing formatting to other text**

1. Select the text that has the formatting you want to copy.

2. On the **Mini Toolbar** or in the **Clipboard** group on the **Home** tab, click the **Format Painter** button once if you want to apply the copied formatting only once, or twice if you want to apply the copied formatting multiple times.

3. Click or select the text to which you want to apply the copied formatting.

4. If you clicked the **Format Painter** button twice, click or select additional text you want to format. Then click the **Format Painter** button again, or press the **Esc** key, to turn off the Format Painter.

Creating WordArt

WordArt provides a method for applying a series of effects to text content. These effects can include outlines, fills, shadows, reflections, glow effects, beveled edges, and three-dimensional rotation. You can use one of the 15 default WordArt styles, modify the effects applied to a WordArt object, or build a combination of effects from scratch. The WordArt color scheme is provided by the document theme.

Become a Microsoft Office Specialist!

When you create a WordArt object, Word attaches it to the active paragraph. Thereafter, you can position the WordArt object independently of the document text.

➤ **To create a WordArt object**

1. On the **Insert** tab, in the **Text** group, click the **WordArt** button.

> **Tip** To create a WordArt object from existing text, select the text before you click the WordArt button.

2. In the **WordArt** gallery, click the style you want.

3. Replace the placeholder text in the WordArt object.

4. Set the size and other attributes of the text as you would with any other text.

➤ **To format the background of a selected WordArt object**

➜ On the **Format** tool tab, do any of the following:

  ○ In the **Shape Styles** gallery, click the built-in style you want to apply.

  ○ In the **Shape Styles** group, in the **Shape Fill**, **Shape Outline**, and **Shape Effects** galleries, click the settings you want.

➤ **To format the text of a selected WordArt object**

➜ On the **Format** tool tab, do any of the following:

  ○ In the **WordArt Styles** gallery, click the built-in style you want to apply.

  ○ In the **WordArt Styles** group, in the **Text Fill**, **Text Outline**, and **Text Effects** galleries, click the settings you want.

  ○ In the **Text** group, click **Text Direction**, and then click the direction in which you want the text to flow.

> **Tip** You change the size, shape, and location of a WordArt object by using the same techniques as you do with other graphic elements.

Setting paragraph indentation and spacing

You can control the position of paragraphs between the document margins by setting the paragraph indentation. You can control individual line and paragraph indentation by setting indents.

- **First Line Indent** The paragraph's first line of text begins at this setting.

- **Hanging Indent** The paragraph's second and subsequent lines of text begin at this setting.

- **Left Indent** The left side of the paragraph aligns with this setting.

- **Right Indent** The paragraph text wraps when it reaches this setting.

When the rulers are displayed, markers on the horizontal ruler indicate the individual indent settings.

A paragraph has internal spacing (the space between the lines within the paragraph, also called *line spacing*) and external spacing (the space before and after the paragraph).

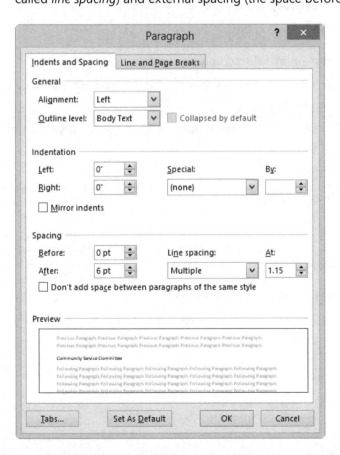

Paragraph spacing is set by the style that is applied to the paragraph. You can modify the paragraph spacing by manually formatting the paragraph, modifying the style, changing the style set, or changing the paragraph spacing setting for the entire document.

➤ **To set the indentation and spacing of selected paragraphs**

1. Display the **Indents and Spacing** page of the **Paragraph** dialog box by doing any of the following:

   ○ On the **Home** tab or **Page Layout** tab, click the **Paragraph** dialog box launcher.

   ○ On the **Line and Paragraph Spacing** menu, click **Line Spacing Options**.

   ○ Right-click a selected paragraph and then click **Paragraph**.

2. In the **Indentation** area, specify the **Left**, **Right**, and **Special** settings.

3. In the **Spacing** area, specify the **Before**, **After**, and **Line spacing** settings. If you want to maintain the line spacing between paragraphs of the same style, select the **Don't add space between paragraphs of the same style** check box.

4. Click **OK** in each open dialog box.

➤ **To set the indentation of selected paragraphs**

→ On the **Home** tab, in the **Paragraph** group, click the **Increase Indent** or **Decrease Indent** button to change only the left indent.

→ On the **Page Layout** tab, in the **Paragraph** group, in the **Indent** area, specify the **Left** or **Right** settings.

> **Tip** To increase or decrease paragraph indentation beyond the margins, specify negative Left and Right settings.

→ On the horizontal ruler, drag the **First Line Indent**, **Hanging Indent**, **Left Indent**, and **Right Indent** markers.

➤ **To set the spacing of selected paragraphs**

→ On the **Page Layout** tab, in the **Paragraph** group, in the **Spacing** area, specify the **Before** or **After** setting.

→ On the **Home** tab, in the **Paragraph** group, click the **Line and Paragraph Spacing** button, and then do one of the following:

- ○ Click **Add Space Before Paragraph**, **Remove Space Before Paragraph**, **Add Space After Paragraph**, or **Remove Space After Paragraph** to change the external spacing. (Only two options will be visible, depending on the current settings of the active paragraph.)
- ○ Click **1.0**, **1.15**, **1.5**, **2.0**, **2.5**, or **3.0** to select a standard line spacing.

➤ **To set paragraph spacing for an entire document**

→ On the **Design** tab, in the **Document Formatting** group, click **Paragraph Spacing** and then click **Default**, **No Paragraph Space**, **Compact**, **Tight**, **Open**, **Relaxed**, or **Double**.

→ On the **Paragraph Spacing** menu, click **Custom Paragraph Spacing**. On the **Set Defaults** page of the **Manage Styles** dialog box, in the **Paragraph Spacing** area, specify the **Before**, **After**, and **Line spacing** settings. Then click **OK**.

➤ **To set the indentation and spacing for all paragraphs of a specific style**

→ Set the indentation and paragraph spacing of an individual paragraph of that style. Then in the **Styles** gallery or pane, right-click the style and click **Update** *style* **to Match Selection**.

Or

1. In the **Styles** gallery or pane, right-click the style, and then click **Modify**.

2. In the **Modify Style** dialog box, on the **Format** menu, click **Paragraph**.

3. On the **Indents and Spacing** page of the **Paragraph** dialog box, do any of the following:

- ○ In the **Indentation** area, specify the **Left**, **Right**, and **Special** settings.
- ○ In the **Spacing** area, specify the **Before**, **After**, and **Line spacing** settings.
- ○ To maintain the line spacing between paragraphs of the same style, select the **Don't add space between paragraphs of the same style** check box.

4. Click **OK** in each open dialog box.

Displaying content in columns

By default, Word 2013 displays the content of a document in one column that spans the width of the page between the left and right margins. You can choose to display content in two or more columns to create layouts like those used in newspapers and magazines.

¶ ══════════════ Section Break (Continuous) ══════════════

Take· a· look· at· how· your· home·is·decorated·and·note· the· things· you· like· and· dislike.·Pay·special·attention· to·the·color·scheme·and·to· how· each· room· "feels"· to· you.·Is·it·inviting?·Does·it·feel· comfortable?· Does· it· relax· you· or· does· it· invigorate· you?¶

Focus· on· the· room(s)· you· would· most· like· to· change.· Brainstorm·all·the·things·you· would·change·in·that·room·if· you· could.· Don't· give· a· thought· to· any· financial· considerations;·just·let·your· imagination·go·wild!·It·might· be·helpful·to·write·down·all· the·negatives·and·positives.· You·don't·need·to·come·up· with· solutions· all· at· once.· Just·be·clear·on·what·you·like· and· what· you· hate· about· that·room.¶

Visit· our· showroom· and· purchase· a· Room· Planner.· While· you're· there,· take· a· look· around· and· see· what·

love,·and·the·rest·will·fall·into· place.¶

Take· your· Room· Planner· home· and· get· to· work!· Adjust·the·planner·so·that·it· models· the· room· dimensions.· Don't· forget· to· place· the· windows· and· doors.·Arrange·the·furniture· placeholders· to· mirror· how· your· room· is· currently· set· up.· Add· the· current· colors,· too.¶

This·is·where·the·fun·begins!· Start·changing·things·around· a· bit.· Move· the· furniture,· add· different· colors,· and· watch· the· room· come· together!· Here's· where· you· can· tell· if· that· rich· red· rug· you· saw· in· the· showroom· enhances· or· overwhelms· your·room.·What·about·that· overstuffed·chair·that·caught· your· eye?· Place· a· furniture· or·accessory·shape,·and·then· color·it.·Does·it·look·great·or· is·it·too·jarring?·Change·the· color...·does·that·help?·Don't·

again.· Does· it· still· look· perfect,·or·is·something·not· quite·right?·You·might·need· to· "live"· with· the· new· plan· for· a· few· days,· especially· if· you've· made· big· changes.· When· everything· feels· just· right·to·you,·you're·ready·for· the·next·big·step!¶

Come·back·to·the·store.·Look· again·at·the·pieces·you·liked· during·your·last·visit·and·see· if·you·still·love·them.·If·you're· not· quite· sure,· go· back· to· your·planner·for·a·little·more· tweaking.· If· you· are· sure,· take·a·look·around·the·store· one· more· time· to· see· if· anything· else· catches· your· eye.· Then· make· your· purchases.· You're· almost· there!¶

NOTE:·If·you·decided·to·paint· your· room,· do· that· before· your· new· pieces· are· delivered.· You'll· want· to· start· enjoying· your· new· room· as· soon· as· your· purchases·arrive.¶

You can format an entire document or a section of a document in columns. When you select part of a document and format it in columns, Word inserts *section breaks* at the beginning and end of the selection to delineate the area in which the columnar format-ting is applied. Content fills the first column on each page and then moves to the top of the next column. When all the columns on one page are full, the content moves to the next page. You can insert *column breaks* to specify where you want to end one column and start another. Section breaks and column breaks are visible when you display for-matting marks in the document.

When dividing text into columns, you can choose one, two, or three columns of equal width or two columns of unequal width. If the standard options don't suit your needs, you can specify the number and width of columns. The number of columns is limited by the width and margins of the page. Each column must be at least a half inch (or 0.27 centimeter) wide.

➤ **To format all the content in a document in multiple columns**

  1. Position the cursor anywhere in the document, but do not select content.

  2. On the **Page Layout** tab, in the **Page Setup** group, click the **Columns** button, and then click the number of columns you want.

➤ **To format part of a document in multiple columns**

  1. Select the contiguous content you want to appear in columns.

  2. On the **Page Layout** tab, in the **Page Setup** group, click the **Columns** button, and then click the number of columns you want.

➤ **To change the width of a section of columns**

  1. Click anywhere in a column. Then on the **Page Layout** tab, in the **Page Setup** group, click the **Columns** button, and click **More Columns**.

  2. In the **Columns** dialog box, do any of the following, and then click **OK**:

      ○ Clear the **Equal Column Width** check box.

      ○ In the **Width and spacing area**, change the **Width** dimensions or the **Spacing** dimensions.

➤ **To display lines between columns**

  → In the **Columns** dialog box, select the **Line between** check box.

➤ **To insert a manual column break**

  → On the **Page Layout** tab, in the **Page Setup** group, click the **Breaks** button, and then click **Column**.

Applying styles to text

Styles are named sets of paragraph and/or character formatting that you can use in place of manual formatting to produce a consistent look throughout a document. There are five types of styles: Character, Paragraph, Linked, Table, and List. The most common types of styles you will use are the following:

- **Paragraph styles** You can use these styles to apply a consistent look to different types of paragraphs, such as headings, body text, captions, quotations, and list paragraphs. Some built-in paragraph styles, such as Heading 1 and Heading 2, are associated with outline levels.

- **Character styles** You can use these styles to change the appearance of selected words.

You can view the available styles in several locations, including the following:

- In the Styles group on the Home tab of the ribbon, the Style gallery displays selected styles. Part of the Style gallery is visible at all times in the Styles group—the number of visible styles depends on the width of your program window and screen resolution. You can scroll through the gallery or expand it to display the entire gallery.

- The Styles pane displays all the currently available styles or a subset thereof that you designate, such as only those that are currently in use. You can display or hide the Styles pane, and from it you can apply and manage all styles.

  In the Styles pane, paragraph styles are identified by a paragraph mark, and character styles are identified by the letter *a*. You can point to any style to display a ScreenTip detailing the formatting included in the style.

- At the left side of a document displayed in Draft view or Outline view, the style area pane displays the name of the style attached to each paragraph. The style area pane does not display character styles. You can display or hide the style area pane.

Style area pane   Styles pane

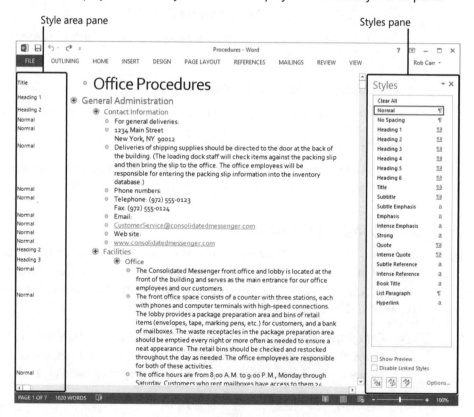

> **See Also** For information about modifying the appearance of styles by changing style sets, see section 1.3, "Format documents."

➤ **To apply a character style**

1. Select the text you want to format, or position the cursor anywhere in a single word you want to format.

2. In the **Styles** pane or **Style** gallery, click the character style you want to apply.

➤ **To apply a paragraph style**

1. Select or position the cursor anywhere in the paragraph you want to format.

2. In the **Styles** pane or **Style** gallery, click the paragraph style you want to apply.

➤ **To modify the content of the Style gallery**

→ To add a style to the **Style** gallery, right-click the style in the **Styles** pane, and then click **Add to Style Gallery**.

→ To remove a style from the **Style** gallery, right-click the style in the **Styles** pane or **Style** gallery, and then click **Remove from Style Gallery**.

➤ **To display the Styles pane in the program window**

→ On the **Home** tab, click the **Styles** dialog box launcher.

➤ **To display visual representations of styles in the Styles pane**

→ At the bottom of the **Styles** pane, select the **Show Preview** check box.

➤ **To display a specific selection of styles in the Styles pane**

1. At the bottom of the **Styles** pane, click **Options**.

2. In the **Style Pane Options** dialog box, click **Recommended**, **In use**, **In current document**, or **All styles** in the **Select styles to show** list.

3. In the **Select how list is sorted** list, click **Alphabetical**, **As Recommended**, **Font**, **Based on**, or **By type**.

4. Select the check boxes for the types of formatting you want to show as styles, and then click **OK**.

➤ **To display the style area pane in a document**

1. Display the document in Draft view or Outline view.

2. Display the **Advanced** page of the **Word Options** dialog box.

3. In the **Display** area, enter a positive number in the **Style area pane width in Draft and Outline views** box. Then click **OK**.

Clearing formatting and styles

From time to time you might want to remove manually applied formatting or styles from document content.

➤ **To clear formatting or styles**

→ To remove manually applied formatting and revert selected content to the settings of the applied styles, press **Ctrl+Spacebar**.

→ To revert selected content to the **Normal** style, do one of the following:

  ○ In the **Styles** pane, click **Clear All**.

  ○ On the **Home** tab, in the **Font** group, click the **Clear All Formatting** button.

→ To revert all content of a specific style to the **Normal** style, in the **Styles** pane, point to the style you want to clear, click the arrow that appears, and then click **Clear Formatting**. The command name indicates the number of instances of the selected style that are currently applied.

> **Tip** The standard methods for clearing formatting don't remove highlighting. To remove highlighting from selected text, on the Text Highlight Color menu, click No Color.

Practice tasks

The practice file for these tasks is located in the MOSWord2013\Objective2 practice file folder. Save the results of the tasks in the same folder.

- In the *Word_2-2* document, display the Navigation pane, and then do the following:

    ○ Select all headings that are formatted as Heading 3 and apply the Heading 2 style to them.

    ○ Apply the Heading 1 style to the *Financial Summary* heading. Then use the Format Painter to apply the same style to the *Financial Statements* and *Statement Notes* headings.

    ○ At the beginning of the document, after the title, select the text *A Brief Review of Our Finances* and format it as a WordArt object of any color. Modify the formatting to include a text outline, text fill, and reflection, but no shadow, glow, bevel, or 3-D rotation effects. Then apply the Triangle Down transform (in the Warp category). Set the width of the WordArt object to 4", position it so that the surrounding text runs behind it, and then center it horizontally on the page.

    ○ Set the paragraph spacing for the entire document to Relaxed.

    ○ Modify the Normal style (in this document only) to indent the first line of each paragraph by 0.5".

    ○ Format the content that follows the *Statement Notes* heading as two columns of equal width, separated by a vertical line. Begin the content of the second column with the *Contingent Liabilities* heading.

Strategy Try to complete all the practice tasks by using as few clicks as possible.

2.3 Order and group text and paragraphs

Managing page breaks

When a document includes more content than will fit between its top and bottom margins, Word creates a new page by inserting a *soft page break* (a page break that moves if the preceding content changes). If you want to break a page in a place other than where Word would normally break it, you can insert a manual page break.

> **Tip** As you edit the content of a document, Word changes the location of the soft page breaks, but not of any manual page breaks that you insert.

➤ **To insert a manual page break**

→ On the **Insert** tab, in the **Pages** group, click the **Page Break** button.

→ On the **Page Layout** tab, in the **Page Setup** group, click the **Breaks** button, and then in the list, click **Page**.

→ Press **Ctrl+Enter**.

➤ **To remove a manual page break**

1. Display formatting symbols.

> **Tip** To display formatting symbols, click the Show/Hide ¶ button in the Paragraph group on the Home tab.

2. Click in the left margin to select the page break paragraph or click to the left of the page break, and then press **Delete**.

➤ **To force a page break before a specific paragraph**

1. Right-click anywhere in the paragraph, and then click **Paragraph**.

2. On the **Line and Page Breaks** page of the **Paragraph** dialog box, in the **Pagination** area, select the **Page break before** check box. Then click **OK**.

> **Tip** If a page break should always appear before a specific type of paragraph, such as a heading, you can incorporate the Page Break Before setting into the paragraph's style.

Managing paragraph breaks

If a paragraph breaks so that only its last line appears at the top of the next page, the line is called a *widow*. If a paragraph breaks so that only its first line appears at the bottom of a page and the rest of the paragraph appears on the next page, the line is called an *orphan*. These single lines of text can make a printed document hard to read, so by default, Word specifies that a minimum of two lines should appear at the top and bottom of each page. As with so many other aspects of the program, however, you can control the way that Word breaks paragraphs and ensure that related paragraphs of information stay together.

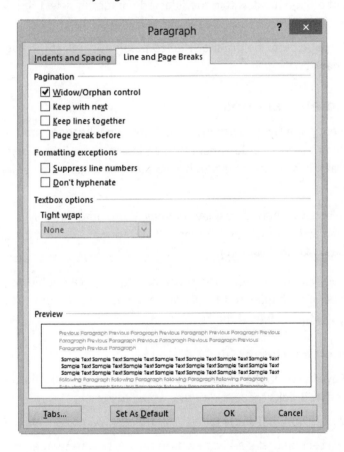

Tip You can apply these options to individual paragraphs, or you can incorporate them into the styles you define for document elements such as headings.

> **To control paragraph breaks**

→ Select one or more paragraphs. On the **Line and Page Breaks** page of the **Paragraph** dialog box, in the **Pagination** area, do any of the following, and then click **OK**:

  ○ To prevent a page break that leaves only one line of the selected paragraph on a page, select the **Widow/Orphan control** check box.

  ○ To prevent a page break after the selected paragraph, select the **Keep with next** check box.

  ○ To prevent a page break within the selected paragraph, select the **Keep lines together** check box.

  ○ To force a page break before the selected paragraph, select the **Page break before** check box.

Creating document sections

You can apply different page layout settings, page numbering, headers and footers, and print options to different parts of a document by creating sections. Sections are separated by section breaks. It is not necessary to have a section break at the beginning or end of a document.

When you format selected content to display columns, Word automatically inserts section breaks before and after the selected content. (If you format an entire document in columns, no section breaks are inserted.)

When formatting marks are displayed, a section break appears as a double dotted line from the preceding paragraph mark to the margin, with the words *Section Break* and the type of section break in the middle of the line.

> **To manually insert a section break**

→ On the **Page Layout** tab, in the **Page Setup** group, click the **Breaks** button, and then in the **Section Breaks** section, click one of the following:

  ○ To create a section that starts content on the next page, click **Next Page**.

  ○ To create a section that starts content on the next even-numbered page, click **Even Page**.

  ○ To create a section that starts content on the next odd-numbered page, click **Odd Page**.

  ○ To create a section that does not affect page breaks, click **Continuous**.

➤ **To specify different settings for a document section**

1. Position the cursor in the section you want to format, and display the settings you want to change.

2. In the **Apply to** list, click **This section**. Then select the settings you want, and click **OK**.

> **Tip** This Section appears in the Apply To list only when the document contains multiple sections.

➤ **To remove a section break**

1. Display formatting marks so that section breaks are visible, if it would be helpful.

2. Drag to select the section break or click to the left of the section break, and then press **Delete**.

Practice tasks

The practice file for these tasks is located in the MOSWord2013\Objective2 practice file folder. Save the results of the tasks in the same folder.

- In the *Word_2-3* document, do the following:
  - ○ Insert a page break before the *Process* heading.
  - ○ In the *Pre-Plan Project* section, select the list items and preceding paragraph. Format each of the selected paragraphs to stay on the same page as the paragraph that follows it.
  - ○ Modify the Normal style so that it does not leave widows or orphans on pages.
  - ○ Create a separate section that contains the *Carry out project* section on its own page. Set the orientation of only this section to Landscape and all four margins of the section to 2".
  - ○ Preview the document on the Print page of the Backstage view to verify the changes.

Objective review

Before finishing this chapter, ensure that you have mastered the following skills:

2.1   Insert text and paragraphs

2.2   Format text and paragraphs

2.3   Order and group text and paragraphs

3 Create tables and lists

The skills tested in this section of the Microsoft Office Specialist exam for Microsoft Word 2013 relate to creating and modifying tables and lists. Specifically, the following objectives are associated with this set of skills:

3.1 Create tables

3.2 Modify tables

3.3 Create and modify lists

Some types of document content are easier to read when presented in a structured format; specifically, in a table or list. Tables are particularly useful for presenting numeric data, but also for organizing text. Numbered lists are an effective means of presenting information that has a specific order or for which you want to designate labels. Bulleted lists present unordered sets of information in a tidy format that is far more legible than running the information together in a long paragraph.

This chapter guides you in studying ways of creating, modifying, and formatting tables, bulleted lists, and numbered lists; sorting table data; and performing calculations in tables.

> **Practice Files** To complete the practice tasks in this chapter, you need the practice files contained in the MOSWord2013\Objective3 practice file folder. For more information, see "Download the practice files" in this book's Introduction.

3.1 Create tables

Creating basic tables

Numeric data can often be presented more efficiently in a table than in a paragraph of text. Tables present large amounts of data, or complex data, in a format that is easier to read and understand by structuring it in rows and columns. Tables frequently include row and column headers to explain the purpose or meaning of the data.

You can create a table in several ways:

- Select the number of rows and columns you want from a grid. Clicking a cell in the grid inserts an empty table the width of the text column. The table has the number of rows and columns you indicated in the grid, with all the rows one line high and all the columns of equal width.

- Specify the number of columns and rows, and the width of the table and its columns, in the Insert Table dialog box.

- Manually draw a table that contains rows and columns of the size you want. The cells you draw connect by snapping to a grid, but you have some control over the size and spacing of the rows and columns. After drawing a table, you can erase parts of it that you don't want and adjust the table, column, and row size by using tools on the Layout tool tab for tables.

> **Tip** When drawing a table, you can display the rulers or gridlines to help guide you in placing the lines.

- Convert selected text to a table of a specified or relative width.

> **Strategy** You can also insert existing data from a Microsoft Excel worksheet in a Word document, but the intricacies of using the Microsoft Office programs together are not likely to be tested on the Word certification exam.

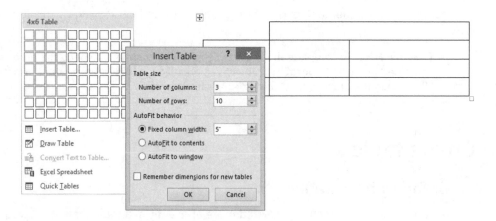

A table appears in the document as a set of cells, usually delineated by borders or gridlines. (In some Quick Tables, borders and gridlines are turned off.) Each cell contains an end-of-cell marker, and each row ends with an end-of-row marker.

> **Tip** Two separate elements in Word 2013 are named *gridlines*, and both can be used in association with tables. From the Show group on the View tab, you can display the *document gridlines* with which you can position content on the page. From the Table group on the Layout tool tab, you can display the *table gridlines* that define the cells of a table.

When you point to a table, a move handle appears in its upper-left corner and a size handle in its lower-right corner. When the cursor is in a table, two Table Tools tabs— Design and Layout—appear on the ribbon.

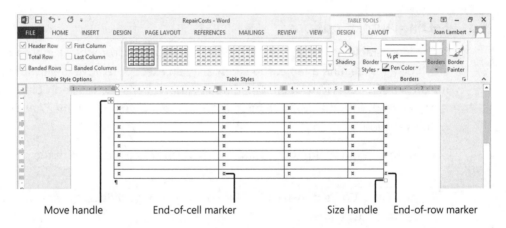

Move handle   End-of-cell marker   Size handle   End-of-row marker

> **Tip** The end-of-cell markers and end-of-row markers are identical in appearance, and are visible only when you display formatting marks in the document. The move handle and size handle appear only in Print Layout view and Web Layout view.

Converting between text and tables

Converting text to a table is particularly easy when the text has a consistent structure, such as that of a tabbed list. You can convert cell entries that are separated by tabs, commas, paragraph marks, or another single character. Similarly, you can convert any table to text that is separated by the same selection of characters.

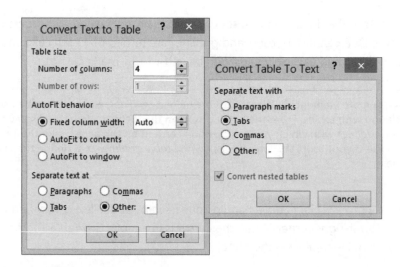

Setting AutoFit options

In the Insert Table or Convert Text To Table dialog box, or from the Layout tool tab at any time after creating a table, you can specify an exact or relative table width by selecting an AutoFit Behavior option. The default AutoFit behavior is Fixed Column Width: Auto, which divides the available page width into equal columns. Other AutoFit Behavior options include:

- Fixed Column Width with a dimension, which creates columns of the specified width.

- AutoFit To Contents, which creates columns only as wide as they need to be to contain their content.

- AutoFit To Window, which sets the table width to the page width and creates equal columns or, when applied to a table that has columns of relative width, maintains the relation.

Nesting multiple tables

Most people are accustomed to thinking of a table as a means of displaying data in a quick, easy-to-grasp format. But tables can also serve to organize your pages in creative ways. For example, suppose you want to display two tables side by side. The simplest way to do this is to first create a table with one tall row and two wide columns and no gridlines. You can then insert one table in the first cell and the other table in the second cell. These nested tables then seem to be arranged side by side.

Payment Schedule	
Interest Rate	3.6%
Years	3
Loan Amount	$155,000.00
Monthly Payment	$4,548.69
Cost of Loan	$163,752.79
3-Year Lease Cost	$180,000.00
Savings	$16,247.21

Payment Schedule	
Interest Rate	5.0%
Years	3
Loan Amount	$155,000.00
Monthly Payment	$4,645.49
Cost of Loan	$167,237.61
3-Year Lease Cost	$180,000.00
Savings	$12,762.39

As with regular tables, you can create a nested table from scratch, by formatting existing information, or by inserting Excel data, and you can format a nested table either manually or by using one of the ready-made table styles.

> **Tip** You can use nested tables to organize a mixture of elements such as text, tables, charts, and diagrams.

➤ **To insert a table**

1. On the **Insert** tab, in the **Tables** group, click the **Table** button.

2. In the grid, move the pointer across and down to select the number of columns and rows you want, and then click the lower-right cell in the selection.

   Or

1. On the **Insert** tab, in the **Tables** group, click the **Table** button, and then click **Insert Table**.

2. In the **Insert Table** dialog box, in the **Table size** area, specify the number of columns and rows you want the table to include.

3. In the **AutoFit behavior** area, do one of the following, and then click **OK**:

   ○ Click **Fixed column width**, and then specify a standard width for the table columns.

   ○ Click **AutoFit to contents** to size the table columns to fit their contents. The width of the resulting table can be less than the width of the page.

   ○ Click **AutoFit to window** to create a table that fits within the page margins and is divided into columns of equal size.

> **To draw a table**

1. On the **Insert** tab, in the **Tables** group, click the **Table** button, and then click **Draw Table**.

2. When the pointer changes to a pencil, drag across and down in the document to define the outer edges of the table or an individual column, row, or cell.

3. Drag to create additional cells, or draw column and row boundaries inside the first cell.

4. Press **Esc** to turn off the table-drawing pointer.

> **Tip** You can add and remove lines from an existing table by using the Draw Table and Eraser commands in the Draw Borders group on the Layout tool tab. You can change the style, weight, and color of the borders of drawn tables by setting the options in the Borders group on the Design tool tab and then using the Border Painter command.

> **To convert selected text to a table**

1. Select the text that you want to convert to a table.

2. On the **Insert** tab, in the **Tables** group, click the **Table** button, and then click **Convert Text to Table**.

3. In the **Convert Text to Table** dialog box, adjust the **Table size** and **AutoFit behavior** settings, select the type of text separator, and then click **OK**.

> **To convert a table to text**

1. Click anywhere in the table.

2. On the **Layout** tool tab, in the **Data** group, click the **Convert to Text** button.

3. In the **Convert Table to Text** dialog box, do one of the following, and then click **OK**:

   ○ Click **Paragraph marks**, **Tabs**, or **Commas** to separate the content of table cells with one of these standard elements.

   ○ Click **Other**, and then enter any single character in the **Other** box to separate the content of table cells with that character.

Inserting preformatted tables

In addition to blank tables and tables converted from text, you can create Quick Tables, which are preformatted tables containing sample data. You can replace the sample data with your own and modify the formatting as you would with any other table.

Built-in Quick Tables include a variety of calendars, simple tables, tables with subheadings, and tabbed lists. Some of the tables present fictitious data for the purpose of illustrating the table layout.

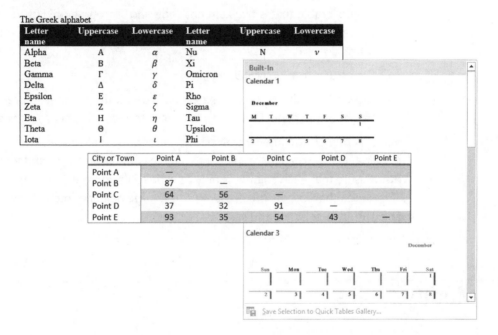

> **Tip** The calendar content of a Quick Table cannot be programmatically set to a specific month and year; that information must be replaced manually. You can create calendars specific to a calendar year or academic year by selecting a calendar template from the New page of the Backstage view.

> **Strategy** You can save your own custom tables (including content) to the Quick Tables gallery so that you can easily insert a frequently used table structure and data into any document. The objective domain for Exam 77-418 includes coverage of inserting preformatted tables. Saving custom building blocks, including Quick Tables, is part of the objective domain for Exam 77-419, Word 2013 Expert.

Practice tasks

The practice file for these tasks is located in the MOSWord2013\Objective3 practice file folder. Save the results of the tasks in the same folder.

- In a new document, create the following tables, separated by page breaks:
  - ○ Create a table that is three columns wide and four rows high. Ensure that each column is exactly 1.5″ wide.
  - ○ Create a table that is five columns wide and six rows high. Ensure that the table is the same width as the page, and the columns are of equal width.
  - ○ Create a Matrix Quick Table.
  - ○ Draw a table that is approximately half the width and one-quarter the height of the page. Divide the table into four columns and six rows.
- In the *Word_3-1* document, convert the tabbed list that follows the *Consultation Fee Schedule* heading into a table with two columns and four rows. Ensure that each column is only as wide as its content. Then convert the information that follows the *In-Home Trip Charge* heading into a page-width table with two columns and six rows.

3.2 Modify tables

Formatting tables

To quickly and professionally format a table, you can apply one of the built-in table styles. These include a variety of borders, shading choices, text colors, and other attributes to give the table a professional look. When formatting a table, you can choose the table elements that you want to emphasize, such as a header or total row or the first or last column, and you can format the table with banded columns or rows to make the contents more legible.

> **Tip** When the edges of table cells are not visually differentiated by borders or other formatting, you can display nonprinting gridlines that define the edges of the table cells.

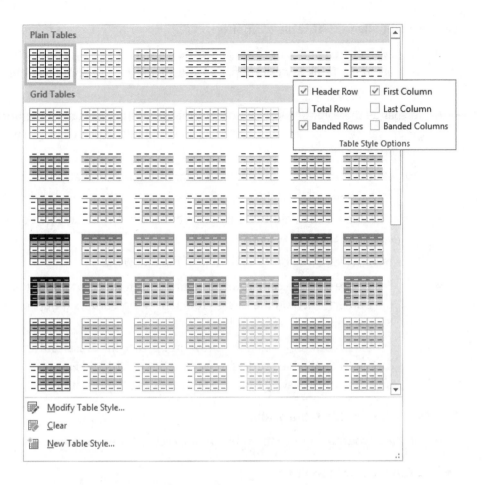

➤ **To apply a built-in table style**

1. Click anywhere in the table you want to format.

2. On the **Design** tool tab, in the **Table Styles** gallery, click the built-in style you want to apply.

➤ **To emphasize table elements**

→ On the **Design** tool tab, in the **Table Style Options** group, select the check boxes of the table elements you want to emphasize.

➤ **To manually format table elements**

→ To shade cells, columns, or rows, select the element and then on the **Design** tool tab, in the **Table Styles** group, click the **Shading** arrow and select the color you want.

→ To change the color or width of borders, on the **Design** tool tab, in the **Borders** group, select the border style, line style, line weight, and pen color you want, and then do one of the following:

○ On the **Borders** menu, click the border configuration that you want to insert with the selected settings.

○ Click the **Border Painter** button, and then click individual table borders to apply the selected settings.

→ To remove selected cell borders, do one of the following:

○ Select one or more cells, rows, or columns from which you want to remove the borders. Then on the **Design** tool tab, in the **Borders** group, on the **Borders** menu, click **No Border**.

○ On the **Layout** tool tab, in the **Draw** group, click the **Eraser** button, and then click individual table borders to remove them. Click the **Eraser** button again, press **Esc**, or click away from the table to turn off the feature.

➤ **To display or hide table gridlines**

→ On the **Layout** tool tab, in the **Table** group, click the **View Gridlines** button.

➤ **To format text in tables**

→ Select the text and format it as you would regular text, by clicking buttons on the **Mini Toolbar** and in the **Font**, **Paragraph**, and **Quick Styles** groups on the **Home** tab.

Modifying table data

After creating a table, you can enter text, numbers, and graphics into its cells. You can edit the information as you would normal text.

Sorting table data

You can sort the data within a table by the contents of one or more table columns. Word sorts only the data rows in your table, and not the header row (if you indicate in the Sort dialog box that the table has one) or the Total row (if you format a Total row in the Table Style Options group).

> **Strategy** Create a table that contains multiple columns and many rows of data and observe the effect of sorting the table by various columns, with and without a header row, and with and without a Total row, to understand the sorting process.

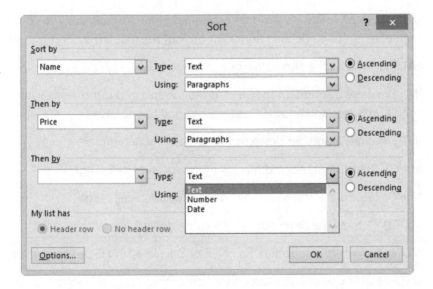

➤ **To sort table data**

1. Click anywhere in the table.

2. On the **Layout** tool tab, in the **Data** group, click the **Sort** button.

3. In the **Sort** dialog box, do the following, and then click **OK**:

   a. In the **Sort by** area, select the primary column by which you want to sort the content, the content type (**Text**, **Number**, or **Date**) if necessary to set the correct numeric sorting order, and **Ascending** or **Descending**.

   b. In the **Then by** area, select and configure up to two additional nested sorting criteria.

Using formulas in tables

When you want to perform a calculation on numbers in a Word table, you can construct a formula by using the tools in the Formula dialog box. In Word 2013 tables, you can create formulas that use the following functions:

- **ABS()** Returns the absolute (positive) value of the specified cell value

- **AND()** Returns the value TRUE if all arguments in the formula are true

- **AVERAGE()** Returns the average value of the specified cell values

- **COUNT()** Returns the number of cells in the specified cell range

- **DEFINED()** Evaluates an argument specified in the formula and returns 1 if the argument has been defined and 0 if it has not been defined or returns an error

- **FALSE()** Returns the alternative output value FALSE

- **IF()** Evaluates a condition specified in the formula and returns one value if the condition is true and another value if the condition is false

- **INT()** Rounds a number down to the nearest whole number

- **MAX()** Returns the maximum value in the specified cell range

- **MIN()** Returns the minimum value in the specified cell range

- **MOD()** Returns the remainder of a division operation

- **NOT()** Returns the opposite of a given or calculated TRUE or FALSE value

- **OR()** Returns one of two values based on criteria specified in the formula

- **PRODUCT()** Returns the product (by multiplication) of the specified cell values

- **ROUND()** Rounds a number to the specified number of digits

- **SIGN()** Returns the value 1 if a number is positive, 0 if the number is zero, or -1 if the number is negative

- **SUM()** Returns the sum (by addition) of the specified cell values

- **TRUE()** Returns the alternative output value TRUE

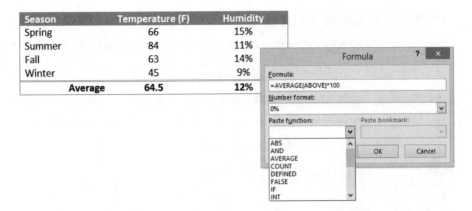

A formula consists of an equal sign (=), followed by a function name, followed by a relative or absolute reference to the cells on which you want to perform the calculation. You can reference the cells as ABOVE, BELOW, RIGHT, or LEFT, or use the cell address or range. The cell address is a combination of the column letter and the row number—for example, A1. Multiple contiguous cells can be addressed as a range consisting of the upper-left cell and the lower-right cell separated by a colon, such as A1:B4.

If you change a value that is used in a formula, you must recalculate the formula.

➤ **To total a column of values in a table**

1. Click the cell in the table where you want the total to appear.

2. On the **Layout** tool tab, in the **Data** group, click the **Formula** button.

3. Enter the formula you want to use in the **Formula** box.

   Or

   In the **Paste function** list, select the function you want to insert. Then enter the cell reference in parentheses and any arguments or values required by the formula.

4. In the **Number format** list, click the output format for the value to append the correct code for that format to the **Formula** box.

5. In the **Formula** dialog box, click **OK**.

➤ **To view and modify table formulas**

→ To display the field codes of a formula rather than its value, right-click the value, and then click **Toggle Field Codes**.

→ To manually recalculate a formula value, right-click the value, and then click **Update Field**.

→ To modify an existing formula, click the formula value, and then on the **Layout** tool tab, in the **Data** group, click the **Formula** button.

Modifying table structure

You can modify a table's structure at any time. The basic ways to do so are as follows:

- Change the height or width of the table, columns, or rows.
- Insert or delete rows, columns, or cells.
- Merge multiple cells into one cell or split one cell into multiple cells.
- Modify the alignment and spacing within cells.

Item	Repair Type	Quantity	Cost in $
Elastomeric Decks	Resurf		
Wood Decks	Replac		
Building Exterior	Repair		
Roof	Resea		
Entry Doors	Repaint	4	600
Carpet	Replace	150 sq. yds.	4,500
Intercom	Replace	1	2,500
Garage Door Opener	Replace	1	2,000
Steel Doors	Repaint	10	750
Exterior Trim	Repaint	800 ft.	4,500
Elevator Hydraulics	Replace	1	55,000
Fire Alarm System	Replace	1	3,000
TOTAL			92,650

Delete Cells...
Delete Columns
Delete Rows
Delete Table

➤ **To select table elements**

→ Click anywhere in the table, column, row, or cell you want to select. On the **Layout** tool tab, in the **Table** group, on the **Select** menu, click **Select Cell**, **Select Column**, **Select Row**, or **Select Table**.

→ To select a table, point to the table, and then click the move handle that appears outside its upper-left corner.

> **Tip** You can move a table by pointing to it and then dragging the handle that appears in its upper-left corner. Or click the handle to select the table, and then use the Cut and Paste commands.

→ To select a row, point to the left border of the row. When the pointer changes to a white, right-pointing arrow, click once.

→ To select a column, point to the top border of the column. When the pointer changes to a black, down-pointing arrow, click once.

→ To select a cell, triple-click the cell or click its left border.

→ To select adjacent cells, click the first cell, hold down the **Shift** key, and then press the arrow keys.

➤ **To display the Table Properties dialog box**

→ Right-click anywhere in the table, and then click **Table Properties**.

Or

1. Click anywhere in the table or select any table element.

2. On the **Layout** tool tab, in the **Table** group, click the **Properties** button.

➤ **To modify properties from the Table Properties dialog box**

→ On the **Table** page, set the table width, specify the way the table interacts with the surrounding text, and access border and shading options, including the internal margins of table cells.

→ On the **Row** page, set the height of the selected rows, whether rows can break across pages (in the event that the table is wider than the page), and whether the header row is repeated at the top of each page when a table is longer than one page.

> **Tip** The Repeat As Header Row option applies to the entire table. The option is available only when the cursor is in the top row of the table. Selecting this option helps readers of a document to more easily interpret data in multipage tables. It also allows assistive devices such as screen readers to correctly interpret the table contents.

→ On the **Column** page, set the preferred width of the selected column or columns.

→ On the **Cell** page, set the width of selected cells and the vertical alignment of text within them. Click the **Options** button on this page to set the internal margins and text wrapping of individual cells.

➤ **To change the size of a selected table**

→ Drag the size handle in the lower-right corner of the table. If you want to maintain the original aspect ratio of the table, hold down the **Shift** key while dragging the size handle.

→ On the **Table** page of the **Table Properties** dialog box, specify the table width in inches or percentage of the available page width, and then click **OK**.

> **Tip** In this book, we specify measurements in inches. You can alternatively use your regional unit of measurement.

➤ **To change the height of a selected row**

→ Drag the row's bottom border up or down.

→ Drag the row's **Adjust Table Row** marker on the vertical ruler up or down.

→ On the **Layout** tool tab, in the **Cell Size** group, change the **Table Row Height** setting.

→ On the **Row** page of the **Table Properties** dialog box, specify the exact or minimum row height, and then click **OK**.

> **Tip** Setting a minimum row height enables the row height to increase when the height of cell content exceeds that measurement. You can set the row height in units such as pixels (px), but Word converts the measurement to inches when you save the changes.

→ With multiple rows selected, click the **Distribute Rows** button in the **Cell Size** group on the **Layout** tool tab, or right-click the selection and then click **Distribute Rows Evenly**.

➤ **To change the width of a selected column**

→ Double-click the column's right border to set it to the narrowest width that fits its content.

→ Drag the column's right border to the left or right.

→ Drag the column's **Move Table Column** marker on the horizontal ruler to the left or right.

→ On the **Layout** tool tab, in the **Cell Size** group, change the **Table Column Width** setting.

→ On the **Column** page of the **Table Properties** dialog box, specify the column width in inches or percentage of the table width, and then click **OK**.

→ With multiple columns selected, click the **Distribute Columns** button in the **Cell Size** group on the **Layout** tool tab, or right-click the selection and then click **Distribute Columns Evenly**.

➤ **To insert rows or columns**

→ Point to the left edge of the table, between two rows where you want to insert another, or to the top of the table between two columns where you want to insert another. A gray insertion indicator labeled with a plus sign appears as you approach a possible insertion point (after any existing row or column). When the insertion indicator turns blue, click to insert the row or column where indicated.

→ Position the cursor in the last cell of a table, and then press **Tab** to extend the table by one row.

Or

1. Click anywhere in a column or row adjacent to which you want to add a single column or row, or select the number of columns or rows you want to insert.

2. On the **Layout** tool tab, in the **Rows & Columns** group, click **Insert Above**, **Insert Below**, **Insert Left**, or **Insert Right**.

Or

On the **Mini Toolbar**, click the **Insert** button, and then click **Insert Above**, **Insert Below**, **Insert Left**, or **Insert Right**.

➤ **To insert cells**

1. Click the cell adjacent to which you want to add a single cell, or select the number of cells you want to insert.

2. On the **Layout** tool tab, click the **Rows & Columns** dialog box launcher.

3. In the **Insert Cells** dialog box, specify how adjacent cells should be moved to accommodate the new cell or cells, and then click **OK**.

➤ **To delete a table, rows, or columns**

1. Click anywhere in the table, row, or column you want to delete, or select the rows or columns you want to delete.

2. On the **Layout** tool tab, in the **Rows & Columns** group, on the **Delete** menu, click **Delete Rows**, **Delete Columns**, or **Delete Table**.

Or

On the **Mini Toolbar**, on the **Delete** menu, click **Delete Rows**, **Delete Columns**, or **Delete Table**.

➤ **To delete cells**

1. Click the cell, or select the cells you want to delete.

2. On the **Layout** tool tab, in the **Rows & Columns** group, click the **Delete** button, and then click **Delete Cells**.

Or

On the **Mini Toolbar**, click the **Delete** button, and then click **Delete Cells**.

3. In the **Delete Cells** dialog box, specify how adjacent cells should move to replace the deleted cell or cells, and then click **OK**.

> ➤ **To create cells that span multiple rows or columns**

→ Select the adjacent cells you want to connect. Then on the **Layout** tool tab, in the **Merge** group, click the **Merge Cells** button.

> ➤ **To divide a selected cell into multiple cells**

1. On the **Layout** tool tab, in the **Merge** group, click the **Split Cells** button.

2. In the **Split Cells** dialog box, specify the number of columns and rows into which you want to divide the cell, and then click **OK**.

> ➤ **To configure the alignment and margins of a selected cell**

→ On the **Layout** tool tab, in the **Alignment** group, click one of the nine **Align** buttons to specify a combination of top, middle, or bottom and left, center, or right alignment.

→ In the **Alignment** group, click the **Cell Margins** button. In the **Table Options** dialog box, set the top, bottom, left, and right margins; specify whether to insert space between cells and how much space to insert; and specify whether to automatically resize cells to fit their contents.

> **Tip** The default cell margins are 0" on the top and bottom and 0.8" on the left and right, with no space between cells and automatic resizing permitted.

Practice tasks

The practice files for these tasks are located in the MOSWord2013\Objective3 practice file folder. Save the results of the tasks in the same folder.

- In the *Word_3-2a* document, do the following:
  - ○ In the Sorting section, sort the table in ascending order by State, then by City, and then by Last Name.
- In the *Word_3-2b* document, do the following:
  - ○ Merge the cells in the first row of the *Estimate* table.
  - ○ Add two rows below the final table row.
  - ○ Change the width of the table to 4".
  - ○ Set the height of the header row to 0.4", and then center-align the contents.

3.3 Create and modify lists

Creating bulleted and numbered lists

Lists are paragraphs that start with a character and are formatted with a hanging indent so that the characters stand out on the left end of each list item. You can create bulleted, numbered, or multilevel lists. You can choose the starting character from a library of preselected bullet symbols, numbering patterns, or multilevel combinations, or you can create your own.

General·Rules¶

1.→Each·Apartment·shall·be·used·for·residential·purposes·only,·except·such·professional·and·administrative·businesses·as·may·be·permitted·by·ordinance,·provided·there·is·no·external·evidence·thereof.¶
2.→No·noxious·or·offensive·activity·shall·be·carried·on,·in,·or·upon·any·Apartment,·Limited·Common·Area,·or·Common·Area;·nor·shall·anything·be·done·therein·which·may·be·an·annoyance·or·nuisance·to·other·residents.¶
3.→No·sports,·activities,·or·games,·whether·organized·or·unorganized,·that·might·cause·damage·to·buildings,·grounds,·facilities,·structures,·or·vehicles,·or·that·are·an·annoyance·or·nuisance,·shall·be·played·in·any·Limited·Common·Area·or·Common·Area.¶
4.→No·Owner·shall·keep·any·animal·within·his·or·her·Apartment·for·any·purpose·other·than·as·a·pet.·The·number·of·cats·and/or·dogs·any·Owner·may·keep·is·limited·to·the·following:¶
  ❖→Two·small·dogs¶
  ❖→Two·cats¶
  ❖→One·cat·and·one·small·dog¶
5.→No·large·dogs·are·allowed,·either·as·pets·of·Owners·or·as·pets·of·visitors.·¶
    a.→Seeing-eye·dogs·may·be·permitted·with·written·approval·of·the·Board.¶
    b.→The·Board·reserves·the·right·to·make·exceptions·to·this·rule.¶
6.→All·pets·must·reside·within·their·Owners'·Apartments.¶
7.→Owners·may·keep·other·types·of·small·pets·that·are·confined·to·aquariums·or·cages.¶
8.→Pets·must·be·on·a·leash·when·in·the·Common·Area.¶

You can format an existing set of paragraphs as a list or create the list as you enter information into the document.

➤ **To create a bulleted list**

1. Enter the list items as separate paragraphs, and then select the paragraphs.

2. On the **Home** tab, in the **Paragraph** group, click the **Bullets** button, or click the **Bullets** arrow and then click the bullet symbol you want to appear before each list item.

   Or

1. Enter * (an asterisk) at the beginning of a paragraph, press the **Spacebar** or the **Tab** key, enter the first list item, and then press **Enter**.

2. Enter items and press **Enter** to add subsequent bulleted items.

3. To end the list, do one of the following:

   ○ To start the next paragraph at the left margin, press **Enter** twice.

   ○ To indent the next paragraph at the same level as the list, press **Enter** and then press **Backspace** or click **None** in the Bullet Library.

Tip If you want to start a paragraph with an asterisk or number but don't want to format the paragraph as a bulleted or numbered list, click the AutoCorrect Options button that appears after Word changes the formatting, and then in the list, click the appropriate Undo option. You can also click the Undo button on the Quick Access Toolbar.

➤ **To create a numbered list**

➜ Select the paragraphs you want to include in the list. On the **Home** tab, in the **Paragraph** group, do one of the following:

   ○ Click the **Numbering** button to apply the standard numbered list format.

   ○ Click the **Numbering** arrow and then click the numbering format you want the list to follow.

   Or

1. Enter *1.* (the number 1 followed by a period) at the beginning of a paragraph, press the **Spacebar** or the **Tab** key, enter the first list item, and then press **Enter**.

2. Enter items and press **Enter** to add subsequent numbered items.

3. To end the list, do one of the following:

   ○ To start the next paragraph at the left margin, press **Enter** twice.

   ○ To indent the next paragraph at the same level as the list, press **Enter** and then press **Backspace** or click **None** in the Numbering Library.

➤ **To create a multilevel list**

1. Select the paragraphs you want to include in the list. On the **Home** tab, in the **Paragraph** group, click the **Multilevel list** button, and then click the format you want the list to follow.

2. To move a list item to a lower level (indented more) press **Tab** at the beginning of the paragraph. To move a list item to a higher level (indented less) press **Shift+Tab** at the beginning of the paragraph.

Modifying bulleted and numbered lists

After you create a bulleted or numbered list, you can modify the content and formatting of the list items, or even change the list type. You can change the bullet symbols, numeric characters, and list item levels, and start or restart list numbering at any value.

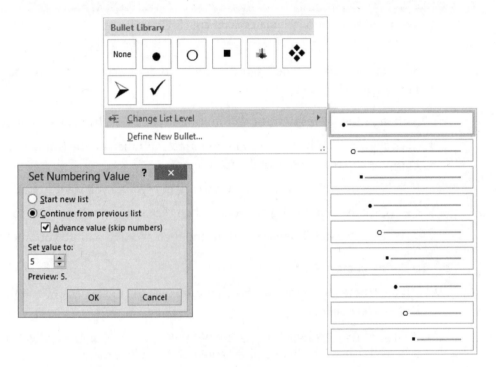

➤ **To change the level of an active list item**

→ On the **Home** tab, in the **Paragraph** group, click the **Increase Indent** button to demote the item or the **Decrease Indent** button to promote the item.

→ On the **Home** tab, in the **Paragraph** group, click the **Bullets** arrow or the **Numbers** arrow, click **Change List Level**, and then in the **Change List Level** gallery, click the level you want.

➤ **To change the order of list items**

→ To move list items, drag them to the new location or cut and paste them. If necessary, click the **Paste Options** button and then click the **Merge List** or **Don't Merge List** button to insert the list item at the hierarchical level you want.

> **Tip** Word automatically updates numbered list items.

→ Sort list items into ascending or descending order by clicking the **Sort** button in the **Paragraph** group on the **Home** tab.

➤ **To change the bullet symbol, numbering style, or multilevel list pattern**

→ Click anywhere in the list you want to format, and then on the **Home** tab, in the **Paragraph** group, do one of the following:

○ Click the **Bullets** arrow, and then click the symbol you want to use.

○ Click the **Numbering** arrow, and then click the symbol you want to use.

○ Click the **Multilevel List** button, and then click the pattern you want to use.

➤ **To define custom bullets**

1. On the **Home** tab, in the **Paragraph** group, click the **Bullets** arrow, and then click **Define New Bullet**.

2. In the **Define New Bullet** dialog box, do one of the following, and then click **OK** to add the bullet to the **Bullet Library** area of the **Bullets** menu.

○ Click the **Symbol** button. In the **Symbol** dialog box, locate and click the bullet symbol you want to use, and then click **OK**.

○ Click the **Picture** button. In the **Picture Bullet** dialog box, locate and click the bullet graphic you want to use, and then click **OK**.

○ If you want to specify a font instead of using the document fonts, click the **Font** button, select the font attributes you want, and then click **OK**.

○ In the **Alignment** list, click **Left**, **Centered**, or **Right** to specify the bullet alignment.

➤ **To define a custom number format**

1. On the **Home** tab, in the **Paragraph** group, click the **Numbering** arrow, and then click **Define New Number Format**.

2. In the **Define New Number Format** dialog box, do any of the following, and then click **OK** to add the number format to the **Numbering Library** area of the **Numbering** menu:

   ○ In the **Number style** list, click the numbering style you want to use.

   ○ If you want to specify a font instead of using the document fonts, click the **Font** button, select the font attributes you want, and then click **OK**.

   ○ In the **Number format** box, enter any characters (such as a period or the word *Level*) that you want to insert before or after the number.

   ○ In the **Alignment** list, click **Left**, **Centered**, or **Right** to specify the number alignment.

➤ **To define a custom multilevel list pattern**

1. On the **Home** tab, in the **Paragraph** group, click the **Multilevel List** button, and then click **Define New Multilevel List**.

2. In the **Define new Multilevel list** dialog box, click the **More** button to display all the list options, if necessary.

3. In the **Click level to modify** list, click the list level you want to modify.

4. If the cursor is currently in a list and you want to format all or part of that list with the new definition, click **Whole list**, **This point forward**, or **Current paragraph** in the **Apply changes to** list.

5. In the **Link level to style** list, click the style to which you want to assign the level you're defining (for example, if you're defining a Level 2 bulleted list item, you might link it to the List Bullet 2 style).

> **See Also** For information about styles, see section 2.2, "Format text and paragraphs."

6. In the **Level to show in gallery** list, click the number of the first level you want to display in the thumbnail on the **Multilevel List** menu. The selected level becomes bold in the preview pane.

> **Strategy** Assigning a name in the ListNum Field List Name box for programmatic use is beyond the scope of Exam 77-418.

7. In the **Number format** area, do either of the following:

    ○ In the **Number style for this level** list, click the numbering style or bullet symbol you want to use for the list level.

    > **Tip** You can define a custom bullet or numbering style by clicking New Picture or New Bullet in the list.

    ○ If you want to specify a font instead of using the document fonts, click the **Font** button, select the font attributes you want, and then click **OK**.

8. If you select a numbering style in the **Number style for this level** list, you can also do the following:

    ○ If you want to prepend the number of a previous level to the selected format, click that level in the **Include level number from** list.

    ○ If you want to specify a starting number or letter other than the default, enter the number or letter in the **Start at** box.

    ○ If you want to ensure that the list numbering does not continue past a specific style (for example, a heading), select the **Restart list after** check box, and then click the style in the associated list.

    ○ If you want to force the use of only Arabic numbers (not Roman numerals), select the **Legal style numbering** check box.

9. In the **Position** area, set the number alignment and text indent for the level.

    Or

    To set an alignment and indent pattern for all levels, click the **Set for All Levels** button. In the **Set for All Levels** dialog box, specify the character and text indent for Level 1, specify the additional indent for subsequent levels, and click **OK**.

10. Repeat the preceding process for each level you want to define. Then click **OK** to add the level definition to the **Lists Library** area of the **Multilevel List** menu.

➤ **To change list or list item indentation**

➜ Drag the indent markers on the horizontal ruler.

> **Tip** You can change both the overall indentation of the list and the relationship of the first line to the other lines.

➤ **To restart the numbering of a numbered list**

➜ Right-click the number of the first list item you want to change, and then click **Restart at 1**.

Or

1. Position the cursor in the list item from which you want to restart. (Subsequent list items will renumber to follow the value you set.)

2. On the **Numbering** menu, click **Set Numbering Value**.

3. In the **Set Numbering Value** dialog box, click **Start new list**, and then click **OK**.

➤ **To continue the numbering of a numbered list**

➜ Right-click the number of the first list item you want to change, and then click **Continue Numbering**.

Or

1. Position the cursor in the first list item you want to change.

2. On the **Numbering** menu, click **Set Numbering Value**.

3. In the **Set Numbering Value** dialog box, click **Continue from previous list**.

4. If you want to skip over numbered lists that are between the original list and the continuation, select the **Advance value** check box and then, in the **Set value to** box, enter the number you want to assign to the list item.

5. In the **Set Numbering Value** dialog box, click **OK**.

Practice tasks

The practice file for these tasks is located in the MOSWord2013\Objective3 practice file folder. Save the results of the tasks in the same folder.

- In the *Word 3-3* document, do the following:
  - ○ Convert the paragraphs under each bold heading other than *The Sequence of Events* to bulleted lists that use the four-diamond bullet character.
  - ○ Create a custom picture bullet that depicts a clip art image of a hero, and apply the bullet to only the list in the section *The Hero*.
  - ○ Convert the paragraphs under the heading *The Sequence of Events* to a numbered list with the *A. B. C.* format. Paste a copy of the numbered list below the original, and restart the numbering of that list, using Arabic numbers instead of letters.

Objective review

Before finishing this chapter, ensure that you have mastered the following skills:

3.1   Create tables

3.2   Modify tables

3.3   Create and modify lists

4 Apply references

The skills tested in this section of the Microsoft Office Specialist exam for Microsoft Word 2013 relate to creating references within document content. Specifically, the following objectives are associated with this set of skills:

4.1 Create endnotes, footnotes, and citations

4.2 Create captions

Word 2013 provides many ways of adding supporting information to a document for the purpose of referencing sources or aiding a reader in locating information.

When you want to provide ancillary information about document content, you can insert footnotes or endnotes in the content that link to that information in another location, usually at the bottom of the page or the end of the document. To indicate the source of content within a document, you can insert citations throughout the content and compile a bibliography based on those citations. In a document that references legal standards, you can mark legal citations within the document and compile a table of authorities from those citations. To clearly indicate the source of images embedded in a document, you can add image captions and optionally compile a table of figures based on the captions.

This chapter guides you in studying ways of creating endnotes, footnotes, bibliographical citations, legal citations, and captions.

> **Practice Files** To complete the practice tasks in this chapter, you need the practice files contained in the MOSWord2013\Objective4 practice file folder. For more information, see "Download the practice files" in this book's Introduction.

4.1 Create endnotes, footnotes, and citations

Inserting footnotes and endnotes

When you insert a footnote or endnote in the text of a document, a reference number, letter, or symbol appears at the insertion location. Your associated note, indicated by the same reference mark, appears in the location that you specify:

- Footnotes can appear at the bottom of the page (relative to the margin) or immediately after the page content. The default location is at the bottom of the page, which provides a consistent experience for readers.

- Endnotes can appear at the end of the document or at the end of the section, if the document contains multiple sections. The default location is at the end of the document.

In most views, footnotes and endnotes are divided from the main text by a note separator line.

"I think," said the little Queen, smiling, "that your friend must be the richest man in all the world."

"I am," returned the Scarecrow. "but not on account of my money. For I consider brains far superior to money, in every way. [1] You may have noticed that if one has money without brains, he cannot use it to advantage; but if one has brains without money, they will enable him to live comfortably to the end of his days." [i]

"At the same time," declared the Tin Woodman, "you must acknowledge that a good heart is a thing that brains cannot create, and that money cannot buy. Perhaps, after all, it is I who am the richest man in all the world."

"You are both rich, my friends," said Ozma, gently; "and your riches are the only riches worth having -- the riches of content!"

The End

---

[i] This is an endnote located at the end of the document.

---

[1] This is a footnote located at the bottom of the page.

A document can contain both footnotes and endnotes. The decision to position a note as a footnote or as an endnote might be governed by your organization's editorial standards, or might simply be a matter of preference. In general, if the associated note contains information that you'd like a reader to be able to immediately reference (such as supporting information), use a footnote; if the note contains information that would be more appropriate gathered with other notes in a central location (such as a source reference), use an endnote.

> **Tip** When inserting notes specifically for the purpose of referencing content sources, use citations instead of endnotes or footnotes. You can then generate a bibliography from the citations. For more information, see "Inserting and referencing citations" later in this section.

➤ **To create a footnote or endnote**

1. Place the cursor in the location from which you want to reference the footnote or endnote.

2. On the **References** tab, in the **Footnotes** group, click the **Insert Footnote** button or the **Insert Endnote** button.

3. In the linked area at the bottom of the page or end of the document or section, enter the note text.

➤ **To set the location of all footnotes or endnotes in a document**

1. Ensure that no footnote or endnote is currently selected.

> **Tip** If a footnote or endnote is selected, the action applies to only the selected element.

2. On the **References** tab, click the **Footnotes** dialog box launcher.

3. In the **Footnote and Endnote** dialog box, do any of the following, and then click **Insert**:

   - In the **Location** area, click **Footnotes** and then, in the associated list, click **Bottom of page** or **Below text**.

   - In the **Location** area, click **Endnotes** and then, in the associated list, click **End of section** or **End of document**.

Modifying footnotes and endnotes

After you insert a footnote or endnote, you can convert it to the other type of note at any time. You can convert either individual notes or all the notes in a document.

By default, footnote reference marks use the *1, 2, 3* number format, and endnote reference marks use the *i, ii, iii* number format. You can change the reference mark system used by either type of note, set the beginning reference mark, and specify the scope of the numbering change.

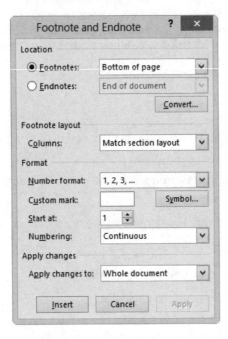

The standard number formats available for both footnotes and endnotes include the following:

- 1, 2, 3, ...
- a, b, c, ...
- A, B, C, ...
- i, ii, iii, ...
- I, II, III, ...
- *, †, ‡, §, ...

You can optionally enter a custom reference mark or select one from the Symbol dialog box.

Numbering options include Continuous, Restart Each Section, and Restart Each Page.

The formatting of reference marks and note text is based on the current document theme. As with other document content, you can also manually format reference marks and note text.

➤ **To change the type of a single footnote or endnote**

➔ Right-click the associated note, and then click **Convert to Endnote** or **Convert to Footnote**.

➤ **To change the type of all footnotes or endnotes**

1. In the **Footnote and Endnote** dialog box, click the **Convert** button.
2. In the **Convert Notes** dialog box, do one of the following, and then click **OK**:
   ○ Select **Convert all footnotes to endnotes** to have only endnotes in the document.
   ○ Select **Convert all endnotes to footnotes** to have only footnotes in the document.
   ○ Select **Swap footnotes and endnotes** to change both types.

➤ **To change the number format of footnotes or endnotes**

1. Ensure that no footnote or endnote is currently selected.
2. In the **Location** area of the **Footnote and Endnote** dialog box, click **Footnotes** or **Endnotes** to indicate the element you want to modify.
3. In the **Format** area, in the **Number format** list, click the number format you want to use.
4. With **Whole document** shown in the **Apply changes to** box, click **Apply** to change all footnotes or endnotes to the new number format.

➤ **To manually format all reference marks or note text**

1. In the document text, select the reference mark for any footnote or endnote.

   Or

   Select the text of any footnote or endnote.
2. On the **Home** tab, in the **Editing** group, click the **Select** button, and then click **Select All Text with Similar Formatting**.
3. Apply the formatting you want.

➤ **To remove a footnote or endnote from a document**

➔ Delete the reference mark.

Inserting and referencing citations

Citations are embedded references to content and information sources from which you can build a reference table or document. A Word document can include two types of citations:

- Citations referencing content sources such as books, magazines, and websites, from which you can build a bibliography

- Citations referencing legal information such as regulations, cases, and statutes, from which you can build a table of authorities

Compiling a bibliography

Many types of documents that you create might require a bibliography that lists the sources of the information that appears or is referenced in the document.

Bibliography

American Bamboo Society. (2010). Retrieved from
    www.americanbamboo.org/BooksOnBamboo.html
Miller, L., & Miller, H. (2012). *Bamboo, Family Style*. Lucerne Publishing.
Nelson, J. (2013). *Big Bad Bamboo*. Litware, Inc.

Whether your sources are books, articles, reports, recordings, websites, interviews, or any of a dozen other types, you can record details about them and then select a common style, such as APA Style (detailed in the *Publication Manual of the American Psychological Association*) or Chicago Style (detailed in the *Chicago Manual of Style*), to have Word automatically reference the sources in that style's standard format.

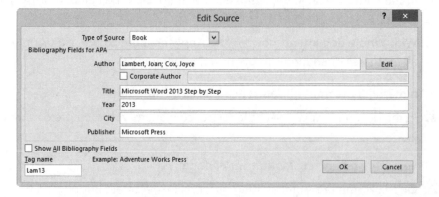

When you create sources, Word stores them in a master list saved in a separate file on your computer's hard disk, so that you can cite them in any document. In the Source Manager dialog box, you can specify the sources that you want to have available to the current document. You can use the Source Manager to help you keep track of sources you use while researching a document, and to ensure that you reference them in the proper format.

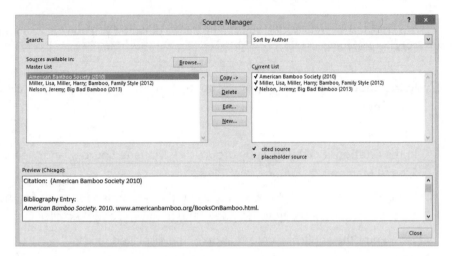

At each location in a document from which you want to reference a bibliographical source, you insert a citation from the Citations & Bibliography group on the References tab.

There are three ways in which you can create and cite sources:

- Provide details for all the sources, and then cite an existing source.
- Provide details for sources as you insert citations.
- Create source placeholders as you insert citations, and then modify the source information in the Source Manager dialog box.

After you enter citations in a document, you can easily compile their sources into a formatted source list, with or without a preformatted heading of *Bibliography*, *References*, or *Works Cited*.

> **Tip** A bibliography includes only cited sources, and does not include source placeholders.

When you compile a bibliography, Word inserts it at the cursor as one field. You can edit the text of a bibliography, but if the source information changes, it is more efficient to edit the source in the Source Manager and then update the bibliography.

➤ **To create a source**

1. On the **References** tab, in the **Citations & Bibliography** group, select the reference style you will be using, if you know it.

> **Tip** The default style is APA. You can retain the default if you don't have another specific preference.

2. In the **Citations & Bibliography** group, click **Insert Citation**, and then click **Add New Source**.

   Or

   In the **Citations & Bibliography** group, click **Manage Sources**, and then in the **Source Manager** dialog box, click **New**.

3. In the **Create Source** dialog box displaying the recommended fields for the selected style, select the source type, do one of the following, and then click **OK**:

   ○ Enter the applicable information in the displayed fields.

   ○ To save additional information about the source, select the **Show All Bibliography Fields** check box, and then enter the information you want.

> **Tip** In the expanded dialog box, the fields recommended for the currently selected style are indicated by red asterisks.

➤ **To create a source placeholder**

1. On the **References** tab, in the **Citations & Bibliography** group, click **Insert Citation**, and then click **Add New Placeholder**.

2. In the **Placeholder Name** dialog box, enter a short name for the source, and then click **OK**.

> **Tip** A source placeholder name cannot include spaces.

➤ **To update a source placeholder**

1. In the **Citations & Bibliography** group, click **Manage Sources**.

2. In the **Source Manager** dialog box, click the placeholder source (indicated by a question mark) in the **Current List** box, and then click **Edit**.

3. In the **Edit Source** dialog box, enter the information that is applicable to the source, and then click **OK** to change the source placeholder to a valid source.

➤ **To cite a source**

1. Position the cursor after the content for which you want to cite the source.

2. In the **Citations & Bibliography** group, click **Insert Citation**, and then click the source or source placeholder.

➤ **To specify a bibliography style**

→ On the **References** tab, in the **Citations & Bibliography** group, click the style you want in the **Style** list.

> **Tip** Changing the bibliography style modifies a source list that has already been inserted in the document.

➤ **To create a bibliography**

1. On the **References** tab, in the **Citations & Bibliography** group, click the **Bibliography** button.

2. In the **Bibliography** gallery, click **Bibliography**, **References**, or **Works Cited** to insert the source list with that heading.

   Or

   On the **Bibliography** menu, click **Insert Bibliography** to insert the source list without a heading.

➤ **To update a bibliography**

→ Click the bibliography field, and then click the **Update Citations and Bibliography** button that appears above the field.

> **Tip** If you used the Insert Bibliography command to compile the source list, the Update Citations And Bibliography button does not appear when you click the field.

→ Right-click anywhere in the bibliography field, and then click **Update Field**.

➤ **To convert a bibliography from a field to text**

→ Click the bibliography field, click the **Bibliography** button that appears above the field, and then click **Convert bibliography to static text**.

Compiling a table of authorities

If a legal document contains items such as regulations, cases, and statutes, you can mark these as legal citations and compile the citations into a table of authorities. In the table, citations are categorized as cases, statutes, rules, treatises, regulations, or other authorities.

Cases

Post v. Jones - 60 U.S. 150 (1856)..5

Smith v. Hooey, 393 U.S. 374 (1969) 2

United States v. Smith, 18 U.S. 5 Wheat. 153 153 (1820) 10, 11

At each location in a document from which you want to reference an authority, you mark a citation from the Mark Citation dialog box, which you open from the Table Of Authorities group on the References tab.

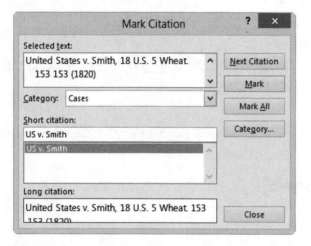

Word uses the citations to create this type of table the same way it uses headings to create a table of contents and captions to create a table of figures. You must insert a citation for each legal reference you want to include, and then generate the table.

> **See Also** For more information about compiling a table of figures, see section 4.2, "Create captions."

➤ **To mark a legal citation**

1. Select the legal reference that you want to mark with a citation.

2. On the **References** tab, in the **Table of Authorities** group, click the **Mark Citation** button to open the **Mark Citation** dialog box.

   Or

   Press **Alt+Shift+I** to open the **Mark Citation** dialog box.

3. In the **Short citation** box, edit the citation to reflect the way you want it to appear in the table.

4. The default category is **Cases**. If you want to change the category, display the **Category** list, and click the category that applies to the citation.

5. To mark one citation, click **Mark**. To mark all citations that match the selected citation, click **Mark All**. Word inserts hidden field codes in the document that identify the citation.

> **Tip** You can leave the Mark Citation dialog box open to facilitate the marking of citations.

➤ **To create a table of authorities**

1. Position the cursor where you want to insert the table of authorities. On the **References** tab, in the **Table of Authorities** group, click **Insert Table of Authorities**.

2. In the **Table of Authorities** dialog box, in the **Category** list, click the category of citations that you want to appear in the table, or click **All** to include all categories.

3. Select formatting options for the table, and then click **OK** to insert the table of authorities.

Practice tasks

The practice file for these tasks is located in the MOSWord2013\Objective4 practice file folder. Save the results of the tasks in the same folder.

- Open the *Word_4-1* document, and do the following:
  - ○ Immediately after the name Jacob, insert an endnote that says *Jacob Grimm lived from 1785-1863.*
  - ○ Immediately after the name Wilhelm, insert an endnote that says *Wilhelm Grimm lived from 1786-1859.*
  - ○ After the name Hanua, insert a footnote that says *Near Frankfurt, in the German state of Hesse.*
- Modify the location of the footnote so that it appears immediately below the text on page 1.
- Convert the endnotes to footnotes, either individually or at the same time.
- Change the footnote numbering format to the range of symbols.
- Reposition the footnotes at the bottom of the page.

4.2 Create captions

Inserting captions

Tables, graphics, and equations—collectively referred to in this context as figures—can be a significant source of information within a document. In most cases, these elements appear inline, near the text that references them. Sometimes, however, it is necessary to reference these elements from other locations. To simplify this process, you can insert figure captions that label each of these elements. You can then easily insert cross-references to the captioned figures.

Image 1: Lake Tahoe provides a scenic backdrop for skiers at Heavenly Ski Resort

The standard number formats available for captions include the following:

- 1, 2, 3, ...
- a, b, c, ...
- A, B, C, ...
- i, ii, iii, ...
- I, II, III, ...

By default, captions use the *1, 2, 3* number format. You can select a different number format for each type of captioned element, if you prefer.

In the caption, the number is preceded by a label of your choice—the default options are Equation, Figure, and Table—or you can create a custom label, such as Image or Map. The number can also incorporate a reference to the current chapter.

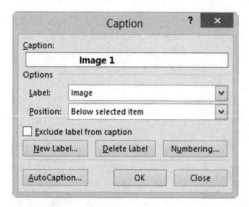

The number assigned to a captioned element is determined by its order in the document. If you caption an element of the same type earlier in the document, the caption numbers that follow, and references to those captions, will update automatically.

> **Tip** The formatting of captions is controlled by the Caption style and changes with the selected document theme elements. Updating the Caption style updates the appearance of all captions.

➤ **To insert a caption**

1. Select the element you want to caption.

2. On the **References** tab, in the **Captions** group, click the **Insert Caption** button.

3. In the **Caption** dialog box, do one of the following:

   ○ To use an existing designator, click it in the **Label** list.

   ○ To create a new designator, click **New Label**. Then in the **New Label** dialog box, enter the label you want to assign to this type of element, and click **OK**.

   ○ To remove the label entirely and use only the number as a caption, select the **Exclude label from caption** check box.

4. In the **Position** list, click **Above selected item** or **Below selected item**.

> **Tip** Use consistent positioning throughout a document to make it easier to read. If the Position list is not available, no item is currently selected.

5. To select a numbering scheme other than the one shown in the **Caption** box, do the following, and then click **OK**:

   a. Click the **Numbering** button.

   b. In the **Caption Numbering** dialog box, in the **Format** list, click the numbering format you want to use.

   c. If you want to incorporate the chapter number or other specifically styled text in the caption, select the **Include chapter number** check box, the name of the chapter number style, and the separator you want to insert between the chapter number and element number.

6. If you want to include a description after the label, click to the right of the label and number in the **Caption** box, press the **Spacebar**, and enter the caption.

7. In the **Caption** dialog box, click **OK**.

➤ **To reference a captioned figure**

1. Position the insertion point in the location in which you want to insert the cross-reference.

2. On the **References** tab, in the **Captions** group, click **Cross-reference**.

3. In the **Cross-reference** dialog box, do any of the following, and then click **Insert**:

   ○ in the **Reference type** list, click the type of item you want to reference (for example, Figure).

   ○ If you want to provide a link to the captioned item, select the **Insert as hyperlink** check box.

   ○ If you want to provide a text reference to the element, select the designator you want to reference (for example, Page Number).

   ○ If you want to include an (above) or (below) designator, select the **Include above/below** check box.

   ○ In the **For which caption** box, click the captioned element you want to reference.

Compiling a table of figures

In a long document that contains many figures, you can help readers locate captioned elements by compiling a table of figures. Unlike a table of authorities, which references all cited authorities in a document divided by type, a table of figures lists only one type of captioned element. Therefore, if you want to list, for example, all equations, figures, and tables in a document, you must create these tables individually.

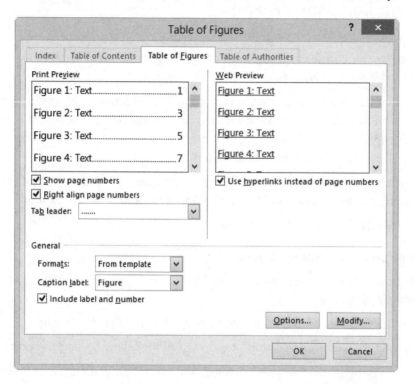

> **To create a table of figures**

1. On the **References** tab, in the **Captions** group, click **Insert Table of Figures**.

2. In the **Table of Figures** dialog box, do any one of the following:

   o To hide page numbers in the table, clear the **Show page numbers** check box.

   o To display page numbers immediately after the captions, clear the **Right align page numbers** check box.

   o To precede page numbers with spaces, hyphens, or underscores rather than periods, select the option you want in the **Tab leader** list.

3. In the **General** area, in the **Caption label** list, click the type of captioned elements you want to display in the table.

4. Do any of the following, and then click **OK**:

- ○ To use a table format other than the default, click **Classic**, **Distinctive**, **Centered**, **Formal**, or **Simple** in the **Formats** list.

- ○ To include only the manually entered description of the captioned elements in the table, clear the **Include label and number** check box.

> **Tip** You can access additional options by clicking the Options or Modify buttons, but these are rarely necessary in a standard Word document.

Practice tasks

The practice file for these tasks is located in the MOSWord2013\Objective4 practice file folder. Save the results of the tasks in the same folder.

- Open the *Word_4-2* document, and do the following:
  - ○ Caption the first graphic as *Figure 1. Man sleeping under apple tree.*
  - ○ Caption the second graphic as *Figure 2. The fox.*
  - ○ Caption the third graphic as *Figure 3. Golden bird in a cage.*

- In the paragraph at the bottom of page 1, after the words *the fox,* insert a set of parentheses. Within the parentheses, insert a hyperlinked cross-reference to Figure 2 that lists only the label and number. To verify that the hyperlink takes you to Figure 2, hold down the Ctrl key and click the link.

- Position the cursor at the end of the document. Below the *Table of figures* heading, insert a table of figures that uses the Distinctive format and lists only the figure descriptions, followed immediately by the page numbers.

- Verify that the hyperlinks from the table of figures work correctly.

- Save the document as *MyGoldenBird*, and then close it.

Objective review

Before finishing this chapter, ensure that you have mastered the following skills:

4.1   Create endnotes, footnotes, and citations

4.2   Create captions

5 Insert and format objects

The skills tested in this section of the Microsoft Office Specialist exam for Microsoft Word 2013 relate to inserting and formatting content objects. Specifically, the following objectives are associated with this set of skills:

5.1 Insert and format building blocks

5.2 Insert and format shapes and SmartArt

5.3 Insert and format images

Professional-looking graphic elements and document parts such as cover pages and sidebars can provide the finishing touches necessary to make a Word document both appealing and useful. Word 2013 provides a wide range of tools that make it easy to create informative, coordinated graphics, graphic elements, and text elements.

This chapter guides you in studying ways of inserting and formatting preformatted document elements known as building blocks, simple shapes, complex business diagrams, and pictures.

> **Practice Files** To complete the practice tasks in this chapter, you need the practice files contained in the MOSWord2013\Objective5 practice file folder. For more information, see "Download the practice files" in this book's Introduction.

5.1 Insert and format building blocks

Building blocks are preformatted text and document elements. There are many types of building blocks. Some are covered in other sections of this book because they fall into the domain of exam objectives other than this one. These include headers, footers, watermarks, and preformatted page numbers (section 1.3, "Format documents"), Quick Tables (section 3.1, "Create tables"), and bibliographies (section 4.1, "Create endnotes, footnotes, and citations").

Other available building blocks include AutoText entries, cover pages, equations, tables of contents, and text boxes. (Text box building blocks include those designed to display sidebars and quotes.) These building blocks are the focus of this section.

Each type of building block is available from its own gallery on the Insert, Design, or References tab of the ribbon, and all are available from the Building Blocks Organizer. Custom building blocks can be made available in the corresponding gallery or in the Quick Parts gallery, which provides easy access to any building blocks you save there. You can also insert document properties and field values (section 2.1, "Insert text and paragraphs") from the Quick Parts menu.

Inserting structural building blocks

Word 2013 includes several types of building blocks that provide structure, which is particularly important for long documents.

- **Cover pages** Inserted at the beginning of a document, a preformatted cover page presents information such as the document title, subtitle, author, company, date, or other information that you want to include. Word 2013 comes with many built-in cover pages, and others are available from the Microsoft Office website.

  A document can have only one cover page; inserting a different cover page replaces the previous version. For this reason, most cover pages display document properties, so they are automatically populated with the correct information.

  You can insert a cover page from any location within a document; Word inserts cover pages only in the correct position, before the first page of the document. A cover page does not have a page number. The page that follows the cover page—the first page of the actual document—remains page 1.

- **Tables of contents** A table of contents at the beginning of a document (after the cover page or title) provides a quick overview of the document's content in addition to an easy way for readers to locate specific document sections.

  Word can automatically generate a table of contents based on the document headings (specifically, the heading levels assigned to styles). By default, a table of contents includes three heading levels, but you can modify the settings to include from one to nine heading levels, choose from various page number leaders or hyperlinks, and select from six styles in addition to the style associated with the template.

> **Strategy** Creating and formatting a table of contents are part of the objective domain for Exam 77-419, "Microsoft Word 2013 Expert," and are not necessary to demonstrate for this exam.

- **Text boxes** To reinforce key concepts and also alleviate the monotony of page after page of plain text, you can insert text boxes designed to hold sidebars and quotes. These preformatted text boxes coordinate with other building blocks (cover pages, headers, footers, and page numbers) to create an extremely professional impression.

  Each text box appears in a specific location on the page and contains placeholder text. You can modify the appearance, location, and content of the preformatted text boxes if they don't quite meet your needs.

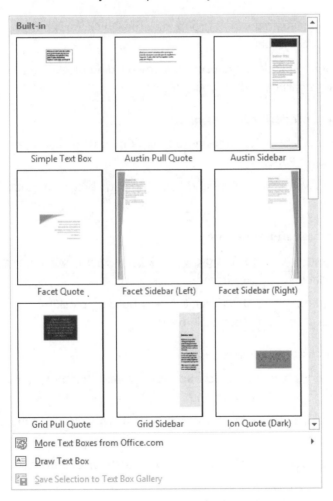

➤ **To insert a predefined cover page**

→ On the **Insert** tab, in the **Pages** group, click **Cover Page**, and then click the cover page you want to insert, or click **More Cover Pages from Office.com** and then click the cover page you want.

> **Tip** Point to a cover page thumbnail to display a ScreenTip that describes the cover page design and its content.

Or

1. On the **Insert** tab, in the **Text** group, click the **Quick Parts** button, and then click **Building Blocks Organizer**.

2. In the **Building Blocks Organizer**, click any building block that is a member of the **Cover Pages** gallery, and then click **Insert**.

➤ **To remove a predefined cover page**

→ On the **Insert** tab, in the **Pages** group, click **Cover Page**, and then click **Remove Current Cover Page**.

→ Select the cover page content and following page break, and then press the **Delete** key.

➤ **To insert a predefined text box**

→ On the **Insert** tab, in the **Text** group, click the **Text Box** button, and then click one of the available text boxes from the gallery.

→ In the **Building Blocks Organizer**, click any building block that is a member of the **Text Boxes** gallery, and then click **Insert**.

➤ **To insert a custom text box**

→ On the **Insert** tab, in the **Text** group, click the **Text Box** button, and click **Draw Text Box**. Then do one of the following:

  ○ Click anywhere on the page to insert a dynamic text box that resizes as you enter text.

  ○ Drag anywhere on the page to draw a text box of a fixed size.

> **Tip** You change the size, shape, and location of a text box by using the same techniques as you do with other graphic elements.

➤ **To copy a text box to a new location**

→ Hold down the **Ctrl** key and drag the text box to the second location.

➤ **To insert text in a text box**

→ Click in the text box so that the text box is surrounded by a dashed (not solid) border. Then enter text as you would in a document.

> **Strategy** Linking text boxes is part of the objective domain for Exam 77-419, "Microsoft Word 2013 Expert," and is not necessary to demonstrate for this exam.

➤ **To change the direction of text in a selected text box**

→ On the **Format** tool tab, in the **Text** group, click the **Text Direction** button, and then click the direction you want.

➤ **To format a text box**

1. Click the text box frame so that the text box is surrounded by a solid (not dashed) border.

2. On the **Format** tool tab, do any of the following:

     ○ In the **Shape Styles** gallery, click the built-in style you want to apply.

     ○ In the **Shape Styles** group, in the **Shape Fill**, **Shape Outline**, and **Shape Effects** menus, click the settings you want.

➤ **To change the default formatting for text boxes**

→ Select a formatted text box, right-click its border, and then click **Set as Default Text Box**.

> **Strategy** Saving selected content as Quick Parts, such as AutoText, is part of the objective domain for Exam 77-419, "Microsoft Word 2013 Expert," and is not necessary to demonstrate for this exam. Neither exam requires you to know how to insert equations.

Managing building blocks

The Building Blocks Organizer contains all the building blocks that are available in the default Building Blocks template (which is available globally) and any other active templates.

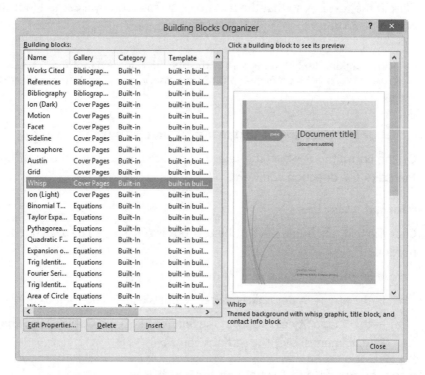

Building blocks can be sorted by name, gallery (type), category (built-in or a custom category that you create), template (storage location), behavior, or description. The names of some building blocks indicate that they belong to a design family, such as Facet or Ion. The behavior setting indicates whether Word inserts the building block in the existing text, in its own paragraph, or on its own page. The description includes information about the building block and, in some cases, recommendations for its use.

> **Tip** To locate a set that includes all the design elements you want to use in the document, sort the list by name to group the building blocks by design family. To identify the alternative locations from which you can insert each type of building block, sort the list by gallery.

➤ **To insert a building block**

→ In the relevant gallery, click the building block you want to insert.

→ Enter the building block name in the document, and then press the **F3** key.

→ In the **Building Blocks Organizer**, click the building block, and then click **Insert**.

Tip You can resize, reposition, or reformat a building block by using commands on the Format tool tab that appears when you select the element.

Strategy Creating, editing the properties of, and deleting building blocks are part of the objective domain for Exam 77-419, "Microsoft Word 2013 Expert," and are not necessary to demonstrate for this exam.

Practice tasks

The practice file for these tasks is located in the MOSWord2013\Objective5 practice file folder. Save the results of the tasks in the same folder.

- Open the *Word_5-1* document, and do the following:
    - Cut the title from the top of the first page, and paste it into the Title property on the Info page of the Backstage view.
    - In the Building Blocks Organizer, locate a design that includes a cover page, header, footer, sidebar, and quote box.
    - Insert a header and footer from the chosen design. Provide a value for each document property specified in the header or footer.
    - On page 3, insert a quote box of the chosen design. Copy the sentence that begins "Don't be impatient" from the paragraph that begins "The children tried very hard" and paste it into the quote box. Ensure that the sentence takes on the formatting of the quote box.
    - On page 4, insert a sidebar of the chosen design. (If the design has an even-page sidebar, use that one.) Cut the last paragraph from the document and paste it into the sidebar.
    - From page 4, insert the coordinating cover page. Provide a value for any document property that doesn't yet have one.
    - Save and close the document.

5.2 Insert and format shapes and SmartArt

Drawing and modifying shapes

If you want to add visual interest and impact to a document but you don't need any-thing as fancy as a picture or a clip art image, you can draw a shape. Shapes can be simple, such as lines, circles, or squares; or more complex, such as stars, hearts, and arrows.

When you finish drawing the shape, it is automatically selected. Later, you can select the shape by clicking it. While the shape is selected, you can move and size it, and you can modify it by using commands on the Format tool tab to do the following:

- Change the shape to a different shape.
- Change the style, fill color, outline, and effects assigned to the shape, including the three-dimensional aspect, or perspective, from which you are observing the shape.

> **Tip** If you change the attributes of a shape—for example, its fill color and border weight—and you want all the shapes you draw from now on in the same document to have those attributes, right-click the shape, and then click Set As Default Shape.

- Specify the position of the shape on the page, and the way text wraps around the shape.

> **Tip** You can manually position a shape by dragging it, or you can select it and press the arrow keys on your keyboard to move the shape in small increments.

- Control the position of the shape in a stack of shapes.
- Specify the shape's alignment and angle of rotation.
- Precisely control the size of the shape.

> **Tip** You can manually change the size and shape of an object by dragging its handles.

You can right-click a shape and click Add Text to place a cursor in the center of the shape. After you enter the text, you can format it with the commands in the WordArt Styles group and control its direction and alignment with the commands in the Text group.

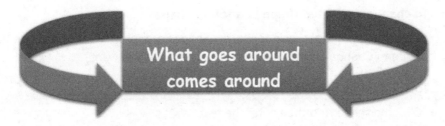

If you build a picture by drawing individual shapes, you can group the shapes so that they act as one object. Then when you move or size the grouped object, the shapes retain their positions in relation to each other. To break the bond, you ungroup the object.

If your picture consists of more than a few shapes, you might want to draw the shapes on a drawing canvas instead of directly on the page. The drawing canvas keeps the parts of the picture together, helps you position the picture, and provides a framelike boundary between your picture and the text on the page. You can draw shapes on the canvas in the usual ways. At any time, you can size and move the drawing canvas and the shapes on it as one unit.

➤ **To draw a standard shape**

   1. On the **Insert** tab, in the **Illustrations** group, click the **Shapes** button.

   2. In the **Shapes** gallery, click the shape you want, and then do one of the following:

   ○ Click anywhere on the page to insert a standard-size shape.

   ○ Drag anywhere on the page to draw a shape the size you want.

➤ **To change the appearance of a selected shape**

   → On the **Format** tool tab, do one of the following:

   ○ In the **Shape Styles** gallery, choose a preformatted style.

   ○ From the **Shape Fill**, **Shape Outline**, and **Shape Effects** menus, apply the style elements you want.

➤ **To change the form of a selected shape**

   1. On the **Format** tool tab, in the **Insert Shapes** group, click the **Edit Shape** button, and then click **Edit Points**.

   2. Drag the intersection points that appear on the shape to change specific vertices, or drag anywhere on the shape border.

> **Tip** You change the size and location of a shape by using the same techniques used to size and move other graphic elements.

➤ **To change a selected shape to another shape**

→ On the **Format** tool tab, in the **Insert Shapes** group, click the **Edit Shape** button, point to **Change Shape**, and then click the shape you want.

➤ **To add text to a selected shape**

→ Click the shape, and then enter the text.

→ Right-click the shape, click **Add Text** or **Edit Text**, and then enter the text.

➤ **To move a selected shape**

→ Drag the shape to a new location and configure its position and layout options.

➤ **To copy a selected shape to a new location**

→ Hold down the **Ctrl** key and drag the shape to the second location.

➤ **To group shapes**

1. Select the first shape, hold down **Ctrl**, and then click the additional shapes you want to group.

2. On the **Format** tool tab, in the **Arrange** group, click the **Group** button, and then click **Group**.

➤ **To ungroup shapes**

1. Select the grouped shapes.

2. On the **Format** tool tab, in the **Arrange** group, click the **Group** button, and then click **Ungroup**.

➤ **To open a drawing canvas**

→ On the **Insert** tab, in the **Illustrations** group, click the **Shapes** button, and then click **New Drawing Canvas**.

Tip If you prefer to always use the drawing canvas when creating pictures with shapes, display the Advanced page of the Word Options dialog box. Then in the Editing Options area, select the Automatically Create Drawing Canvas When Inserting AutoShapes check box, and click OK.

Controlling shape layout options

By default, Word inserts a shape in front of the surrounding text, and other graphic objects in line with the surrounding text. You can change the position of the object on the page and the way text wraps around it.

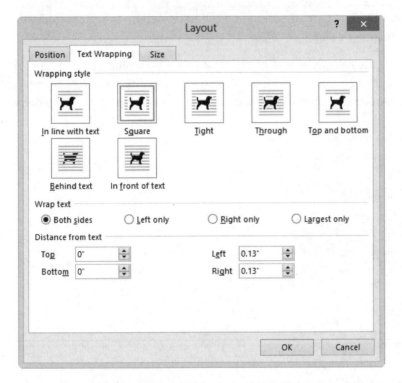

The text wrapping options specify the relationship of the object to the text and include:

- **In Line with Text** The line spacing increases as necessary to accommodate the object. The bottom of the object aligns with the bottom of the text on the same line.

- **Square** The text wraps to the leftmost and rightmost points of the object.

- **Tight** The text wraps closely to the left and right edges of the object.

- **Through** The text wraps as closely as possible to all edges of the object.

- **Top and Bottom** The text flows above and below the object, but the space to its left and right are left clear.

- **Behind Text** The text flows in front of the object without interruption.

- **In Front of Text** The text flows behind the object without interruption.

When you choose a text wrapping option other than In Line With Text, you can specify that an object be positioned in one of two ways:

- **Absolutely** This option positions the object at a distance you set from a margin, page, column, character, paragraph, or line.

- **Relatively** This type of positioning is determined by the relationship of the object to a margin or page.

You can take the guesswork out of setting an object's position by choosing one of nine predefined position options from the Position gallery. These options all implement square text wrapping in a specific location relative to the margins of the page.

Even if you use one of the predefined options to position an object, you can move the object manually by dragging it to another position on the page. Often it is easier to drag objects into position if you display an on-screen grid to align against. You can also use alignment commands to align objects with the margins and with each other.

Changing the document text after you position an object might upset the arrangement of content on the page. On the Position page of the Layout dialog box, you can specify whether an object should move with its related text or remain anchored in its position. You can also specify whether the object should be allowed to overlap other objects.

After you arrange objects on the page, you can hide and display them by clicking the Visible icons in the Selection pane, so that you can judge each object's contribution to the whole.

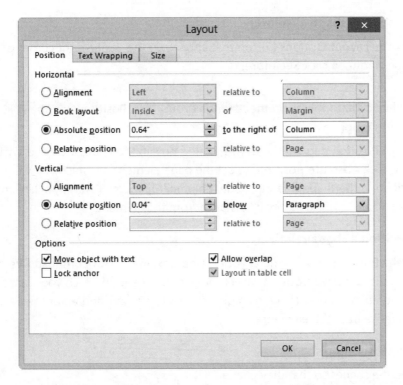

If you insert several objects and then position them so that they overlap, they are said to be "stacked." The stacking order (which object appears on top of which) is initially determined by the order in which you inserted the objects, but it can also be determined by other factors such as the type of text wrapping assigned to each object. Provided all the objects have the same kind of text wrapping, you can change their order by selecting an object and clicking the Bring Forward or Send Backward button in the Arrange group to move the object to the top or bottom of the stack. If you click either button's arrow and then click Bring Forward or Send Backward, the object moves forward or backward in the stack one position at a time.

➤ To control the flow of text around a selected shape

→ Click the **Layout Options** button that appears in the upper-right corner of the shape, and then click the text wrapping option you want.

→ On the **Format** tool tab, in the **Arrange** group, click **Wrap Text**, and then click the wrapping style you want.

➤ **To position a shape absolutely**

1. Click the **Layout Options** button that appears in the upper-right corner of the shape, and then click **See more**.

   Or

   On the **Format** tool tab, in the **Arrange** group, click **Position**, and then click **More Layout Options**.

2. On the **Position** page of the **Layout** dialog box, in the **Horizontal** and **Vertical** sections, click **Absolute position**, select the page element on which you want to fix the position of the shape (Margin, Page, Column, Character, Paragraph, Line, or specific margin), and enter the specific distance from the element.

➤ **To position a shape relatively**

→ On the **Position** page of the **Layout** dialog box, in the **Horizontal** and **Vertical** sections, click **Relative position**, select the page element on which you want to fix the position of the shape (Margin, Page, or specific margin), and enter the percentage difference from the element.

➤ **To stack multiple shapes**

→ Drag the shapes so that they overlap.

➤ **To change the stacking order of multiple shapes**

1. Select the shape you want to move up or down in the stack.

2. On the **Format** tool tab, in the **Arrange** group, do any of the following:

   ○ Click the **Bring Forward** or **Send Backward** button to move the shape up or down one level.

   ○ In the **Bring Forward** list, click **Bring to Front** to move the shape to the top of the stack.

   ○ In the **Bring Forward** list, click **Bring in Front of Text** to move the shape on top of the surrounding text.

   ○ In the **Send Backward** list, click **Send to Back** to move the shape to the bottom of the stack.

   ○ In the **Send Backward** list, click **Send Behind Text** to move the shape behind the surrounding text.

➤ **To display the Selection pane**

→ On the **Format** tool tab, in the **Arrange** group, click the **Selection Pane** button.

→ On the **Home** tab, in the **Editing** group, click **Select**, and then click **Selection Pane**.

Inserting and modifying SmartArt graphics

When you want to clearly illustrate a concept such as a process, cycle, hierarchy, or relationship, the powerful SmartArt Graphics tool makes it easy to create dynamic, visually appealing diagrams. By using predefined sets of coordinated formatting and effects, you can almost effortlessly construct any of the following types of diagrams:

- **List** These diagrams visually represent lists of related or independent information—for example, a list of items needed to complete a task, including pictures of the items.

- **Process** These diagrams visually describe the ordered set of steps required to complete a task—for example, the steps for getting a project approved.

- **Cycle** These diagrams represent a circular sequence of steps, tasks, or events, or the relationship of a set of steps, tasks, or events to a central, core element—for example, the looping process for continually improving a product based on customer feedback.

- **Hierarchy** These diagrams illustrate the structure of an organization or entity—for example, the top-level management structure of a company.

- **Relationship** These diagrams show convergent, divergent, overlapping, merging, or containment elements—for example, how using similar methods to organize your email, calendar, and contacts can improve your productivity.

- **Matrix** These diagrams show the relationship of components to a whole—for example, the product teams in a department.

- **Pyramid** These diagrams illustrate proportional or interconnected relationships—for example, the amount of time that should ideally be spent on different phases of a project.

- **Picture** These diagrams rely on pictures instead of text to create one of the other types of diagrams—for example, a process picture diagram with photographs showing the recession of glaciers in Glacier National Park. Picture diagrams are a subset of the other categories but are also available from their own category so that you can easily locate diagram layouts that support images.

SmartArt graphic layouts are available from the Choose A SmartArt Graphic dialog box. The categories are not mutually exclusive, meaning that some layouts appear in more than one category. Word 2013 includes some new built-in SmartArt templates, in addition to an internal connection to additional templates on the Office website.

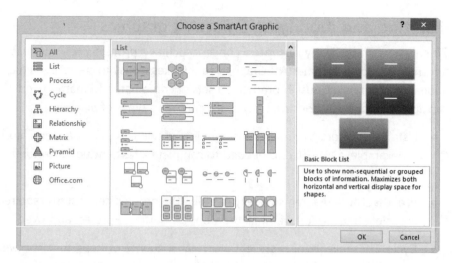

After you choose a layout, Word inserts the basic diagram into the document, and some-times displays the associated list format in the Text pane, into which you can enter infor-mation. (If the Text pane doesn't open automatically, you can display it by clicking the button on the left edge of the diagram.) You can enter more or less information than is required by the original diagram; most diagrams support a range of entries (although a few are formatted to support only a specific number of entries). You can insert and mod-ify text either directly in the diagram shapes or in the associated Text pane. The selected layout determines whether the text appears in or adjacent to its shapes.

> **Tip** You change the size, shape, and location of a SmartArt graphic by using the same techniques as you do with other graphic elements.

After you create a diagram and add the text you want to display in it, you might find that the diagram layout you originally selected doesn't precisely meet your needs. You can easily change to a different diagram layout without losing any of the information you entered in the diagram. If a particular layout doesn't support the amount or level of information that is associated with the diagram, the extra text will be hidden but not de-leted, and will be available when you choose another layout that supports it.

> **Tip** If a gallery has a sizing handle (three dots) in its lower-right corner, you can drag the handle upward to reduce the height of the gallery. You can then display more of the document and the gallery at the same time.

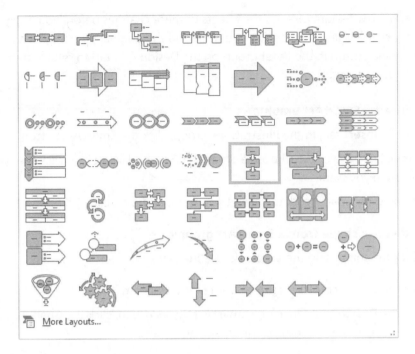

When you decide on the layout you want to use, you can add and remove shapes and edit the text of the diagram by making changes in the Text pane, or by using the options on the SmartArt Tools tabs.

You can make changes such as these by using the commands on the Design tool tab:

- Add shading and three-dimensional effects to all the shapes in a diagram.
- Change the color scheme.
- Add shapes and change their hierarchy.

> **Tip** You can rearrange shapes by dragging them.

You can customize individual shapes in the following ways by using the commands on the Format tool tab:

- Change an individual shape—for example, you can change a square into a star.
- Apply a built-in shape style.
- Change the color, outline, or effect of a shape.
- Change the style of the shape's text.

The Live Preview feature displays the effects of these changes before you apply them. If you apply changes and then decide you preferred the original version, you can click the Reset Graphic button in the Reset group on the Design tool tab to return to the unaltered diagram layout.

➤ **To insert a SmartArt graphic**

1. On the **Insert** tab, in the **Illustrations** group, click the **SmartArt** button.
2. In the left pane of the **Choose a SmartArt Graphic** dialog box, click the type of diagram you want.
3. In the center pane, click the layout you want, and then click **OK**.

➤ **To delete a shape from a SmartArt graphic**

→ Click the shape, and then press the **Delete** key.

➤ **To change the color scheme of a selected diagram**

→ On the **Design** tool tab, in the **SmartArt Styles** group, click the **Change Colors** button, and then click the color scheme you want.

➤ **To apply a style to a selected diagram**

→ On the **Design** tool tab, in the **SmartArt Styles** gallery, click the style you want to apply.

➤ **To apply a style to a selected diagram shape**

→ On the **Format** tool tab, in the **Shape Styles** gallery, click the style you want to apply.

Or

1. On the **Format** tool tab, click the **Shape Styles** dialog box launcher.
2. In the **Format Shape** pane, on the **Fill & Line**, **Effects**, and **Layout & Properties** pages, choose the effects you want to apply.

Strategy Many formatting options are available from the Design and Format tool tabs. Be familiar with the options available on the tool tabs and in the associated dialog boxes.

Practice tasks

The practice file for these tasks is located in the MOSWord2013\Objective5 practice file folder. Save the results of the tasks in the same folder.

- Open the *Word_5-2* document, and do the following:
  - In the blank area below the story, use no fewer than three shapes to draw a character from the story. Size, color, and arrange the shapes as necessary. When you finish, group the shapes into one object.
  - Position the grouped shapes to the right of the second paragraph, and wrap the text squarely to the left of the shapes.
  - In the blank area below the story, create a SmartArt graphic that diagrams the process that occurs in the story. Include at least four events from the story.
- Save and close the document.

5.3 Insert and format images

Inserting images

You can insert digital photographs or pictures created in almost any program into a Word document. You specify the source of the image you want to insert by clicking one of these two buttons, which are located in the Illustrations group on the Insert tab:

- **Pictures** Click this button to insert a picture that is saved as a file on your computer, on a network drive, or on a device (such as a digital camera) that is connected to your computer.

- **Online Pictures** Click this button to insert a royalty-free clip art image from Office.com, a web search result from Bing, or an image stored on your Microsoft OneDrive or another online source.

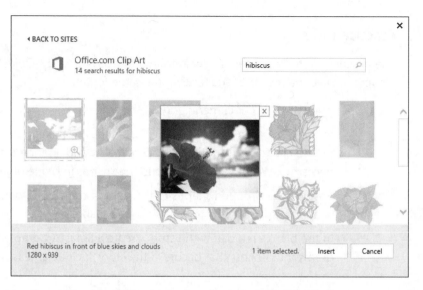

You can also capture and insert images of content displayed on your computer screen directly from Word. By using the built-in screen clipping tool, you can insert screen captures of entire windows or selected areas of on-screen content.

> **Strategy** Tasks related to inserting charts, screenshots, screen clippings, apps, or media are not necessary to demonstrate for this exam.

➤ To insert an image from a file

1. On the **Insert** tab, in the **Illustrations** group, click the **Pictures** button.

2. In the **Insert Picture** dialog box, browse to and click the file you want. Then do one of the following:

   - Click **Insert** to insert the image into the document.

   - In the **Insert** list, click **Link to File** to insert an image that will update automatically if the image file changes.

   - In the **Insert** list, click **Insert and Link** to insert an image that you can manually update if the image file changes.

➤ **To insert an online image**

1. On the **Insert** tab, in the **Illustrations** group, click the **Online Pictures** button.

2. In the **Insert Pictures** window, click the online source (Office.com, Bing Image Search, a Microsoft SharePoint site or OneDrive folder, or one of the available linked third-party sites).

3. Enter a keyword in the search box and press **Enter**, or navigate to the picture you want to insert.

4. Double-click the image you want to insert.

> **Tip** You change the size, shape, and location of an image by using the same techniques as you do with other graphic elements.

Formatting images

After you insert an image in a document, you can modify it in many ways. For example, you can crop or resize an image, change the image's brightness and contrast, recolor it, and apply artistic effects to it. You can apply a wide range of preformatted styles to an image to change its shape and orientation, in addition to adding borders and picture effects.

You modify the image by using commands on the Format tool tab, which is displayed only when an object is selected.

- The Adjust group contains commands that enable you to change the image's brightness and contrast, recolor it, apply artistic effects to it, and compress it to reduce the size of the document containing it.

- The Picture Styles group offers a wide range of picture styles that you can apply to an image to change its shape and orientation, and add borders and picture effects. This group includes the Quick Styles gallery, which contains many preformatted styles that you can apply very quickly.

- The Arrange group contains commands for specifying the relationship of the image to the page and to other elements on the page.

- The Size group contains commands with which you can crop and resize images.

The Picture Styles group offers a wide range of picture styles that you can apply to an image to change its shape and orientation and add borders and picture effects. You can select a preset style or select individual border, effects, and layout settings. Effect options include shadow, reflection, glow, soft edge, bevel, and rotation effects.

The Artistic Effects gallery provides many preformatted effects designed to make a photograph appear more like a watercolor or pastel painting, mosaic, or chalk or pencil sketch.

In addition to changing the style of an image, you can crop or resize it, recolor it, and compress it to reduce the size of the document containing it. Changing an image's brightness, contrast, or color is done by choosing options on the Picture page of the Format Picture pane. You can make precise adjustments to the image's size by selecting options on the Size page of the Layout dialog box or in the Crop section of the Picture page of the Format Picture pane.

➤ **To apply a style to a selected image**

→ On the **Format** tool tab, in the **Picture Styles** group, expand the **Quick Styles** gallery, and then click the style you want to apply.

Or

1. On the **Format** tool tab, click the **Picture Styles** dialog box launcher.

2. In the **Format Picture** pane, on the **Fill & Line**, **Effects**, **Layout & Properties**, and **Picture** pages, choose the settings you want to apply. Then click **Close**.

➤ **To apply artistic effects to a selected image**

→ On the **Format** tool tab, in the **Adjust** group, expand the **Artistic Effects** gallery, and then click the effect you want to apply.

➤ **To apply picture effects to a selected image**

→ On the **Format** tool tab, in the **Picture Styles** group, click **Picture Effects**, point to any category to expand the gallery, and then click the effect you want to apply.

➤ **To change the brightness, contrast, or color of a selected image**

→ In the **Format Picture** pane, on the **Picture** page, modify the settings in the **Picture Corrections** and **Picture Color** sections.

➤ **To change the size and/or shape of a selected image**

→ Drag its sizing handles.

→ On the **Format** tool tab, in the **Size** group, change the **Height** and **Width** settings.

→ On the **Format** tool tab, click the **Size** dialog box launcher. Then on the **Size** page of the **Layout** dialog box, change the **Height**, **Width**, or **Scale** settings.

> **Tip** You change layout options for images by using the same techniques as you do with other graphic elements.

Practice tasks

The practice files for these tasks are located in the MOSWord2013\Objective5 practice file folder. Save the results of the tasks in the same folder.

- Open the *Word_5-3a* document, and do the following:
  - ○ Position the cursor at the beginning of the second paragraph, and insert the *Word_5-3b* picture.
  - ○ Apply styles and effects to the picture so that it appears to depict a painting of a princess in an oval frame.
  - ○ Resize the picture so that it is 2.5 inches wide, and maintain the original aspect ratio.
  - ○ Position the picture in the exact center of the page, and wrap the text tightly around it.
  - ○ Save and close the document.

Objective review

Before finishing this chapter, ensure that you have mastered the following skills:

5.1 Insert and format building blocks

5.2 Insert and format shapes and SmartArt

5.3 Insert and format images

Index

A

absolute positioning
  building blocks, 141
  objects, 146
  shapes, 148
alignment
  paragraph, 4
  table, 92
appending content, to current document, 64
artistic effects, applying, 156, 157
authors
  adding to Author property, 43
  removing from Author property, 44
AutoCorrect
  adding text shortcuts, 70
  inserting text and symbols, 69
AutoFit, setting options, 94

B

backward compatibility, maintaining, 54
bibliographies
  converting from fields to text, 125
  creating, 122, 125
  source placeholders, 124
  sources, 124, 125
  specifying styles for, 125
  updating, 125
bookmarks
  creating, 18
  inserting, 18
  moving, 19
borders
  changing in paragraphs, 4
  changing in tables, 100
  removing, 100
breaking columns manually, 22
breaking lines automatically, 23
brightness, changing in images, 157
building blocks
  behavior settings, 140
  for cover pages, 136
  formatting, 141
  for tables of contents, 136
  inserting in documents, 141

  positioning, 141
  resizing, 141
  sorting by behavior, 140
  structural, 136
  for tables of contents, 136
  templates, 140
Building Blocks Organizer, 138
bulleted lists, creating, 109
bullets, changing/defining, 112

C

calculations in tables, 102, 103
captioned figures, referencing, 131
captions
  inserting, 130
  number formats, 129
  referencing figures, 131
cells. *See* table cells
character styles, 81, 83
characters, formatting, 4, 26
citations
  See also legal citations
  creating bibliographies, 122
  creating sources, 124
Clipboard, 4
  managing items by using, 63
  pane, displaying, 62
color schemes, changing in diagrams, 152
colors, changing in images, 157
column breaks, 22, 81
columns
  See also table columns; text columns
  aligning gridlines, 92
  breaking, 22
  changing section widths, 81
  displaying content in, 80
  displaying lines between, 81
  formatting text into, 22
commands
  adding to custom groups, 41
  for formatting images, 155
  managing keyboard shortcuts for, 46
  not visible on ribbon, 39
  removing from groups, 41
Compatibility Checker, 56

R

S

W

watermarks
  adding text, 32
  inserting, 31
  using pictures as, 32
Windows Explorer. *See* **File Explorer**
WordArt, 75, 76
words. *See* text

X

XPS (.xps) files, 53

Z

Zoom group, 35
Zoom slider, 36
zooming, 36

About the author

Joan Lambert has worked in the training and certification industry since 1997. As President of Online Training Solutions, Inc. (OTSI), Joan is responsible for guiding the translation of technical information and requirements into useful, relevant, and measurable training and certification tools.

Joan is a Microsoft Office Certified Master, Microsoft Certified Application Specialist Instructor, Microsoft Certified Technology Specialist, Microsoft Technology Associate, Microsoft Certified Trainer, and the author of more than two dozen books about Windows and Office (for Windows and Mac). Joan enthusiastically shares her love of technology through her participation in the creation of books, learning materials, and certification exams. She greatly enjoys communicating the benefits of new technologies by delivering training and facilitating Microsoft Experience Center events.

Joan currently lives in a small town in Texas with her simply divine daughter, Trinity, their two slightly naughty dogs, naturally superior cat, vast assortment of fish, and the super-automatic espresso machine that runs the house.

Online Training Solutions, Inc. (OTSI)

OTSI specializes in the design, creation, and production of Microsoft Office, SharePoint, and Windows training products for information workers and home computer users. For more information about OTSI, visit *www.otsi.com*.

The team

This book would not exist without the support of these hard-working members of the OTSI publishing team:

- Rob Carr
- Susie Carr
- Joyce Cox

- Jeanne Craver
- Kathy Krause
- Marlene Lambert

- Jaime Odell
- Candace Sinclair
- Jean Trenary

We are especially thankful to the support staff at home who make it possible for our team members to devote their time and attention to these projects.

Rosemary Caperton provided invaluable support on behalf of Microsoft Press.

Now that you've read the book...

Tell us what you think!

Was it useful?
Did it teach you what you wanted to learn?
Was there room for improvement?

Let us know at http://aka.ms/tellpress

Your feedback goes directly to the staff at Microsoft Press,
and we read every one of your responses. Thanks in advance!